"A powerful and insightful read that elucidates how the armor of God can empower and equip every believer, regardless of where they are in their Christian journey. This book takes the modern-day theologian on a mindful and spiritual journey that engages the intellect and builds on the tenets of the armor of God needed to stand firm in their faith."

—**Lieta Lynnette Singleton**, Ordained Preacher & Elder of the AME Zion Church, New York

"To accessorize something is 'to add elements that enhance its beauty and appeal.' Doris Bourgeois Turner has masterfully applied this concept to the spiritual realm, offering a profound and thought-provoking perspective. As I reflect on her insights, I am compelled to consider: How can I better accessorize my life in Christ? In her introduction, Turner poses a compelling question: 'Can we enhance our inner selves, our Christian character, and our lifestyles in ways that build up the body of Christ?' This inquiry is explored with remarkable depth, and a powerful response unfolds in chapter 2. Yet, before reaching that point, Turner provides an unflinching reminder in chapter 1 that disobedience to God carries life-altering consequences. From the garden of Eden to the present day, its impact is evident. How, then, do we move forward? The answer lies in adorning ourselves with the word of God, embracing its truths, internalizing its wisdom, and allowing it to transform us from the inside out. Colossians 3:16–17 exhorts us to let the message of Christ dwell richly within us. To perpetuate this spiritual 'accessorization,' we must be vigilant: guarding our speech, monitoring our spiritual health, cultivating Christlike attitudes, and ensuring that sin is not given a foothold in our hearts. This work by Doris Bourgeois Turner is an invaluable resource for every believer seeking to grow in grace and reflect the beauty of Christ in every area of life."

—**VIRGINIA P. HAYES**, President, Woman's Auxiliary, National Baptist Convention

"This book reveals the truth about what life would be like when you disobey God's word. Navigating this life without being in the will of God will cause you not to partake in the many blessings God has stored up for you. Being in the educational system for the past ten and a half years, we reward good manners, good behaviors, and respect. This is similar to how God will reward his children when they are obedient to his will and his way. Doris A. Bourgeois Turner presents 'Consequences for Disobedience: Life-Altering' to the reader, offering a clear understanding of the instructions and expectations that must be followed in order to live a life pleasing to God. I love the term 'accessories for godly living,' referring to having compassion, kindness, humility, gentleness, and patience, all the recipes of living Christlike. This is truly an awesome book."

—**FELICIA MOORE JONES**, Elementary School Secretary, Louisiana

"Doris Bourgeois Turner has written an encouraging, inspiring, and engaging book on how believers should be obedient to God's expectations and the consequences for disobedience in their relationship with God. It is appropriate to accessorize the outer self, but God is more concerned about the believer's inner self. Furthermore, Turner encourages believers to put away negative behaviors, as noted in 1 Pet 2:1–3, such as malice, deceit, and envy. Instead, believers should crave 'the pure spiritual milk' of God's word to help them grow spiritually. *Accessorization* is about the believer's plight, encompassing the causes of separation from God's will and fellowship, which include loss of blessings, divine judgment, adverse outcomes, and spiritual death. She informs believers about the essentiality of taking the path of repentance and being accountable for their actions, which is crucial on their journey with God. Turner reminds us that sin earns the life-altering consequence of death. This will help believers grow spiritually by increasing their faith in their journey with God. This book is a must-read."

—**JEAN MARIE JOSEY**, Spiritual Advisor, New York

Accessorization

Accessorization

*God's Expectations of Believers—
Consequences for Disobedience*

Doris A. Bourgeois Turner

Foreword by Joe Albert Bush Sr.

WIPF & STOCK · Eugene, Oregon

ACCESSORIZATION
God's Expectations of Believers—Consequences for Disobedience

Copyright © 2026 Doris A. Bourgeois Turner. All rights reserved. Except for brief quotations in critical publications or reviews, no part of this book may be reproduced in any manner without prior written permission from the publisher. Write: Permissions, Wipf and Stock Publishers, 199 W. 8th Ave., Suite 3, Eugene, OR 97401.

Wipf & Stock
An Imprint of Wipf and Stock Publishers
199 W. 8th Ave., Suite 3
Eugene, OR 97401

www.wipfandstock.com

PAPERBACK ISBN: 979-8-3852-6589-3
HARDCOVER ISBN: 979-8-3852-6590-9
EBOOK ISBN: 979-8-3852-6591-6

VERSION NUMBER 02/06/26

All Scripture quotations, unless otherwise indicated, are taken from the Holy Bible, New International Version (NIV). Copyright © 1973, 1978, 1984, 2011 by Biblica, Inc. Used by permission of Zondervan Bible Publishers. All rights reserved worldwide. www.zondervan.com. The "NIV" and "New International Version" are trademarks registered in the United States Patent and Trademark Office by Biblica, Inc.

Scriptures marked KJV are taken from the KING JAMES VERSION (KJV), which is in the public domain.

Scripture quotations identified NKJV are taken from the New King James Version (NKJV). Copyright © 1982 by Thomas Nelson. Used by permission. All rights. Reserved.

Scripture quotations identified NLT are taken from the Holy Bible, New Living Translation (NLT): Scripture taken from the Holy Bible, New Living Translation, Copyright © 1996, 2004, 2015 by Tyndale House Publishers, Inc., Carol Stream, Illinois 60188. All rights reserved, and used by permission.

This book is dedicated to my husband, Reverend Dr. Johnny Turner, for his prayers, love, patience, and support.

It is dedicated to my bonus children: Reverend Lieta Lynnette Mallory Singleton, Kimberly Denise Mallory, Donnette, Jeffrey, Jennifer, and Jonathan Turner. As your bonus mom, I thank you for your love, respect, and support. I am deeply grateful to my church sister, Charlie Sue Graham, who shared her home and family with me, and to my church niece, Joyce Patterson, and church daughter, Carole Burgess, for their love, devotion, and sincerity as we journeyed through life.

I am also dedicating this book to the best and most formidable teachers who taught me about love, sharing, support, forgiveness, and God's incredible grace and mercy. These two teachers were our parents, the late Earlean and Leroy (LeRoyal) Bourgeois Sr. They taught the four of us—the late Leroy Jr., and my sisters, Alberda and Lois, and me—"always to have each other's backs and keep God at the center of everything we do."

Contents

Foreword by Joe Albert Bush Sr. | ix
Acknowledgments | xi

Introduction: God's Expectations of Believers in the Body of Christ | 1
1. Consequences for Disobedience: Life-Altering | 11
2. Accessorizing Your Christian Character and Self-Absorbed Nature (Temperament) in the Body of Christ | 23
3. The Spiritual Ingredient Mix for Accessorizing Your Temple | 88
4. Jesus's Perfect Invitation Leads to Expectations for Eternal Life | 123

Epilogue | 129

Bibliography | 133
Scripture Index | 137

Foreword

DORIS A. BOURGEOIS TURNER gives the people of God and the body of Christ a beautiful gift in *Accessorization: God's Expectations of Believers—Consequences for Disobedience*. This book is especially for those with a sincere desire to make a positive impact on the kingdom through their lifestyle.

I am honored to have been asked to write the foreword for this book, authored by a licensed social worker, a certified dean of Christian education in her local district association, and the wife of a retired pastor.

This book is a road map for those who take discipleship seriously enough to understand that the call of Christ is nothing short of a call to model a new way of life, demonstrated by obedience to the principles of faith.

As a pastor of nearly fifty years (forty-three of those years in New York City, the largest and most culturally diverse city in the United States), I have witnessed some parishioners make tremendous strides in their journey toward spiritual maturity. At the same time, I have watched others who evidence little to no progress in their spiritual growth and development. I have observed that people who appreciate that the God who calls us in Jesus Christ is a God of high standards always seem to make the most significant progress. Such people also have the most tremendous impact on building God's kingdom here on earth.

Doris A. Bourgeois Turner skillfully uses the Scriptures of the Old and New Testaments, along with events from her own life experience, to underscore the truth that the God who calls us expects us to live by standards. She also stresses that failure to accessorize one's Christian character properly can have life-altering consequences for the believer.

Stressing the importance of parents, educators, and others in leadership positions, Doris B. Turner promotes the careful watch of one's tongue and the guarding of personal emotions, such as anger, vengeance, hostility, and resentment. She emphasizes a positive self-image and a biblically centered personal demeanor as ways in which the Christ-follower should be adorned to reflect the life of Christ properly.

This book is a must-read for those who desire to deepen their spiritual life or sharpen their personal witness, but it would also be an excellent tool for small-group Bible study and reflection. The reader is sure to come away more prepared to model the life of obedience.

Rev. Dr. Joe Albert Bush Sr.
Master of Divinity, Lutheran Theological Southern Seminary, South Carolina; a Doctor of Ministry degree, Drew University Theological Seminary, New Jersey; CEO and Executive Director of EVEN SO SEND I YOU and Senior Pastor of Walker Memorial Baptist Church, Bronx, New York.

Acknowledgments

I OWE SO MUCH to my parents, Leroy (LeeRoyal) and Earlean Bourgeois, for their encouragement, support, and sacrifice throughout my childhood, high school, undergraduate studies at Grambling State College, now Grambling State University, Grambling, Louisiana, and during graduate studies at the State University of New York School of Social Welfare, Albany, New York.

Their intercessory prayers were offered to God to bless, keep, and guide each of their four children as we traveled life's highway, striving to make the best decisions to enhance our lives and lifestyles. Although our parents did not have much, they utilized whatever God blessed them with to help us enjoy life better than they did. They instilled in us an understanding and appreciation of what God did for them, and the importance of always remembering from whence we came. I give notable accolades to them.

I am also profoundly thankful for the unwavering prayers, love, support, and encouragement of my sisters, Alberda M. Bourgeois and Lois A. Bourgeois Cassamier, and acknowledge the significant impact of my late brother, Leroy Jr. I am grateful and blessed to have had two of my high school classmates assist me along the early stage of my journey—Clementine Martin, who utilized her typing skills when I could not type or did not own a typewriter, and Ella Mae Jenkins, who drove me to Grambling, Louisiana, to be interviewed for a scholarship to attend graduate school at the State University of New York School of Social Welfare, Albany, New York. I owe a debt of gratitude to the individual

Acknowledgments

who purchased the ticket, making it possible for me to fly to Albany, New York. I humbly appreciate their kindness and generosity. I also wish to acknowledge my spiritual advisor, Evangelist Jean Marie Josey, whose intercessory prayers and words of wisdom have been a constant source of strength and guidance; Reverend Gertrude Harris, with her quiet demeanor and words of wisdom; Sister D, "It is better to be asked up then to be asked down"; as well as Mother Geneva Norman, a compassionate, caring, genuine prayer warrior; and Mother Mildred Ephron, who always said, "Dar dar, baby, always have faith and continue to trust in the Lord; he knows." Other great women of God, now transitioned from labor to rest, were spiritual sources, providing guided direction and words of profound wisdom: the late Mothers Isabella F. Martin, Doris M. Brooks, Cornelia Gordon Graham, and Evangelist Andrea L. Allen. Lastly, I am grateful for the continuous love, support, and encouragement of my wonderful husband, Reverend Dr. Johnny Turner, an author in his own right. I give all glory, honor, and praise to God, who keeps, guides, and directs me, and has placed such wonderful people in my life, giving me the privilege of meeting and spending time with them on my spiritual journey. Their wisdom and knowledge have enriched my life in ways I could never have imagined.

Introduction
God's Expectations of Believers in the Body of Christ

Various Scriptures have been studied to help believers understand God's expectations and standards for them, as well as how they must conduct themselves in diverse settings and continue to be role models for others. In Col 3:12–14, the specific standards, not the physical but the spiritual, is laid out for all believers. It begins by letting believers know that as God's chosen people, holy and clearly loved, "they must clothe themselves with compassion, kindness, humility, gentleness, and patience." These could clearly be labeled as "accessories" for godly living. Believers are further instructed to bear with each other and forgive whatever grievances they may have against another person. In other words, believers do not harbor angry feelings and emotions, but must, as Scripture tells us in verse 13, "forgive as the Lord forgave us." A critical accessory, in verse 14, is love, "and over all these virtues we must put on love as God commands," which is the binding agent that pulls everything together in "perfect unity," just as outfits use various accessories to pull them together so that the wearer looks fashionable. God provides the peace of Christ in the believer's heart, but the heart must be clean and pure, and it does not lend itself to transgressions that would block a clear and direct connection to the Vine. God's word must dwell within each believer, just as the Holy Spirit guides and directs the path of those who trust and believe in his word and his power.

Accessorization

Accessorization, in relation to God's expectations and commands, pertains to how believers adorn themselves in both their outer appearance and inner virtues. An individual may look great on the outside, the in-vogue look, but their inner appearance and character are not pleasing to God. Believers are encouraged to focus on virtues and those accessories that reflect the newness of Christ, the new person, rather than on elaborate clothing, expensive jewelry, hairstyles, or beautiful fingernails, which can be changed in a moment's notice.

While the foundation for God's standards was laid out in the Old and New Testaments, he expects you to be perfect; the Hebrew word *"Tamim"* is translated as "perfect," "finished," or "complete before the Lord," as commanded by Moses in the book of Deuteronomy. The Greek word *"teleios"* refers to wholeness. God made you in his image, flawless and complete. Matthew 5:48 (KJV) states, *"Be ye therefore perfect, even as your Father which is in heaven is perfect."* Some individuals may not have a believer's perspective or an awareness of God's love and how he allowed the sacrifice of his only Son, Jesus Christ, as the ultimate gift for their salvation and eternal life. You can inspire others and bring them closer to God's love through your positive behavior and moral and spiritual development. This inspiration and closeness to God's love must be your driving force and motivation for positive behavior, moral development, and spiritual growth.

God always has expectations and standards for his children and made it possible for you to be acceptable to him at all times when he gave you "righteousness as our clothing," as found in Job 29:14. Righteousness, from a biblical perspective, means "being acquitted or vindicated," and only through your faith in Jesus Christ does God regard you as righteous. With your righteous clothing, God no longer sees your sin. Imagine if God held believers accountable for all the things they did that were not visible to the naked eye. Where would you be without his forgiveness, grace, and mercy?

As a believer, you can see good manners, respect, obedience, and positive attitudes as essential accessories in the body of Christ.

Introduction

As children growing up with adult role models, many of you witnessed family members displaying appropriate manners, such as saying "thank you" and "please," and showing respect, especially to older individuals, by using phrases like "yes, ma'am" or "no, ma'am." However, some of you may be products of dysfunctional families and were not exposed to positive family living or the positivity that comes with a family environment. Teachers and leaders in school and the faith community play a crucial role in shaping the behavior of children and adults. They serve as the conduit for immediate positive feedback for expressing good manners, respect, and other acceptable social behaviors. It is easy to focus on the negative and become critical and intolerant when mistakes are made. However, these mistakes must not be overlooked; instead, they must be corrected in a positive and compassionate manner, which will help build self-confidence, self-esteem, and a positive self-image. You must remember that some families have been and may continue to be exposed to excessive negativity, which can become overwhelming. As leaders and educators, you are responsible for guiding and supporting these individuals, empowering them to make positive life changes. It becomes the responsibility of leaders, teachers, and Christian educators to set good moral and spiritual examples for children, adolescents, and one another. Good skills, abilities, manners, and values are learned through familial socialization and interaction. However, many family structures are disrupted by social, economic, educational, and other cultural factors. These challenges to family structures should evoke your empathy and understanding, motivating you to provide the necessary support and guidance to those in need.

Lack of good manners is a growing problem among some children and adults, whether in homes, schools, or places of worship such as churches. We should teach believers to modify their speech habits by using "yes" instead of "yeah" or "what" and consistently use "thank you" and "please" to foster courtesy and graciousness in speech. How do you, as believers, exhibit accessorized good manners in diverse settings? Are separate and distinct manners appropriate for conducting oneself in church versus

Accessorization

other social settings, such as school or work? It sometimes seems as though social graces have become a thing of the past. The term "accessorizing," is pertinent to your lives and your children's. "Social grace is inner discipline and joy. These are the birthright of the human being who has been allowed to develop essential human qualities."[1] Dressing in a way that aligns with your personal style boosts your self-esteem and allows you to embrace your individuality.[2] Using accessories to enhance an individual's outer appearance or inner self-conception aims to increase inner awareness or consciousness.

As parents, leaders, and teachers, you must prioritize good manners and conduct, especially in your homes, as the foundation for teaching and training your children. This training is conducted during religious services at your church and during school-related activities, such as riding public transportation, using the school bus, or walking home. God's eyes are constantly watching you, hearing your every conversation, and knowing your wise or deceptive plans before you execute them. In the clothing industry, accessorizing means taking immense pride in ensuring that your garments are complemented or supplemented with the appropriate fashion accessories. Why do you accessorize? Is it to accentuate the current styles and attire you may already be comfortable with, or could it be a mechanism to hide insecurities and imperfections, or perhaps the fear of exposing inner truths to humanity?

Accessorizing makes you feel more comfortable, helps you look and feel younger, boosts your self-esteem, and enhances your self-image, ultimately leading to increased self-confidence. By following the trendiest fashion in such an uncomplicated way, you know you look good. It doesn't matter what anyone else thinks or says; self-confidence says, "Girl Gone!" You know you've got it. You look so sophisticated. A repeated fashion trend from earlier years may suggest "I am doing my thing." There has been a recent surge in the popularity of false eyelashes. This fashion trend is back with a vengeance; the longer, the better; the blacker, the

1. Montessori, "Social Grace."
2. Jackson, *Art of Accessorising*, 8.

Introduction

more attractive, with a particularly sexy look; and the thicker, the more fashionable. "You know, girl, you got it going on"—a repeated fashion trend from years earlier during my youth. The longer, darker, and curlier the lashes are at the ends, the more they signify a specific look. These sisters know they've "got it going" by their smiles and manners. And you can't tell the Sistas they don't look great. Through their cheerful outlook and style, they know they look good. Another returning fashion trend is wearing long, beautiful, colorful, decorative fingernails. Sometimes, I see Sistas with extremely long nails, and I say, "I know you don't cook or do housework, and most definitely, you don't wash dishes!" She may laugh and say, "Girl, but not with these nails. It costs too much money." While in the supermarket, I observed cashiers trying to touch various keys on the register at checkout. Depending on her demeanor, facial expression, and body language, I may say, "Wow, what nice nails! Aren't you afraid you will get their tip caught in that machine?" She may respond, "I am careful not to break them." Of course, in my silent thoughts and wonderful smile, and my lips are not moving, I am saying that if they were shorter, you could work faster, and this line would move more quickly. But I hold my tongue (the bit of fire) these post-COVID days; I am more cautious and wiser about what I say and to whom.

    Many people reference some societal issues and challenges as being related to side effects from COVID and frequently use the term "COVID brain," which is a colloquial term for "Brain fog."

> Brain fog is a collection of neurocognitive impairments reported to be one of the most debilitating problems experienced by people with Long COVID, a condition in which COVID-19-like symptoms continue or develop after the acute infection has passed.
>
>   It is considered a Long COVID symptom, a condition that can affect anyone who has had COVID-19 and can last up to eighteen months or longer. The symptoms reportedly include slowed or sluggish thinking, difficulty processing information, forgetfulness, and inability to focus, concentrate, or find the right words in a

Accessorization

conversation. People with brain fog are also reported to experience depression, anxiety, and mood components.[3]

I have become more cautious, patient, observant, and less likely to get involved in issues than in earlier years. If people stopped for a few minutes and thought about the situation and the consequences of their actions, they would calm their spirits before running home and getting a gun to make a point or resolve an issue. Once the trigger is ignited, the bullet leaves the chamber; it is all over; the bullet cannot be returned. Life for all people involved has been altered, and the challenges that followed suggest that the situation could have been resolved more effectively. If the person had just reflected for a moment, maybe they would not be sitting in jail with the possibility of life imprisonment or on death row. Now, where do they go from here? What challenges lie ahead? They could have been believers, but anger and frustration evolved into rage and fury due to life circumstances. And for what purpose? Did the quick-temper action prove or resolve anything? No, it did not. Everyone involved in the circumstances has had their life-altered.

From a believer's perspective, how do you access Christ? Can you enhance your inner self, your Christian character, and lifestyle to build up the body of Christ? How does your temperament, attitude, behavior, and emotion contribute to your self-confidence and self-assurance, complementing your spiritual lifestyle? How do you control and calm your tongue from speaking harsh words that cut at the individual's core? As one senior saint often said, "Speaking what is on her mind, she was not going to hold all those emotions inside of her, making her ill; she was going to tell it like it is." What impact does "telling it like it is" have on the audience? Do young people hear this statement as a positive way to resolve an issue? The tongue and its bit of spark are in motion. How do you soothe the hurt and pain you experience from cutting your tongue? From a biblical perspective, how do believers know the proper fix and expectations for you? How do you understand fitting compliments, such as love, praise, compassion, commitment,

3. Katella, "Long COVID Brain Fog."

Introduction

and appreciation, for your spiritual garment? What is the "fix-it" or "merge" button for easing spiritual disturbances, distractions, and duplication of issues and concerns? On my cell phone, in my contact folder, there is a "Fix-It Merge" button. If there are duplicate contacts, I receive a notice asking if I want to merge or fix them. If I say yes, the duplicates are merged immediately or discarded, providing consistency and clarity with the contact list. As a believer, can you mix your spiritual accessories with worldly ones? Can you add or mix worldly texture to your spiritual pattern so you don't appear as a dull believer? What does God expect of you when you live in a world where some believers think it is OK to have fun at a club or bar on Saturday night by adding a little spirit flavor to their orange or cranberry juice? After all, Jesus turned water into wine at the great wedding feast; this is the statement often heard when alcohol is introduced into a conversation. How do you become as conscious about your spiritual awareness as you are about your physical accessorizing? Just as the world offers guidance on accessorizing, so does the Holy Bible regarding dressing your inner self and your outer appearance. From a biblical perspective, you can dress modestly and with self-control. First Peter 1:2 instructs us to focus on developing a gentle and quiet spirit, which is more precious to God than outward adornment. God, regarding Saul, made his instructions very clear to Samuel about a man's outer appearance: "Don't judge him by his appearance or height, for I have rejected him. The Lord doesn't see things the way you see them. People judge by outward appearance, but the Lord looks at the heart" (1 Sam 16:7 NLT). While humans spend an enormous amount of time accessorizing their outer appearance, which is not essential to God, how much of their time is spent on building, accessorizing, or purifying their inner self, which is necessary and more important to God?

In Mic 6:8, one can read God's requirements for you to be just and fair in your interactions and dealings with others, whether they are believers or not. He further expects you, as members in the body of Christ, to be kind and caring toward others as he is toward you and, above all, compassionate and forgiving toward

Accessorization

those in your immediate circle and those not included in it. Yours is to be a spirit of humility in thought and action, just as you walk in humbleness, portraying Christlikeness. As you read God's word daily, you strive to pattern your lifestyle after Christ's, recognizing that God does not accept haughtiness and indignant behavior. He does not appreciate rudeness, jealousy, or the pain experienced by those of you who let your heart lead you to the source of your self-accessorization. He does not appreciate those of you who become avengers by taking matters into your own hands; God tells you in Rom 12:19 (KJV), "Dearly beloved, avenge not yourselves, but rather give place unto wrath: for it is written, Vengeance is mine; I will repay, saith the Lord." Romans 12:21 (NLT) clearly states, "Don't let evil conquer you, but conquer evil by doing good."

You love, understandably, so keep your heart pure so that God's Holy Spirit will continue to dwell in your temple and minister to you as you are confronted by a barrage of ungodliness, not of Christ. In addition, through the Holy Spirit, God has provided every believer with nine characteristics or principles designed to help you wade through the pain of the heart. Proverbs 4:23 tells you that God expects you to guard your heart with his Spirit so that your heart will continue to be tender, as God's mercies proclaim. Sometimes, life's challenges can make you hardened and embittered. As further mentioned in Bible Hub, "A hardened heart is a spiritual condition characterized by insensitivity and resistance to God's voice and guidance."[4] As you struggle with accessorization, remember that God provided you with sixty-six books in the Bible, offering a pathway to righteous living. With the situation in your hands, you are subject to failure and unfairness to others; however, in the hands of God, he forgives you for your shortcomings and gives you greater direction through the guidance of the Holy Spirit. However, you must allow self-will to diminish while God's will take root.

I am authoring my book during the 2024 presidential campaign. For the first time in history, a sitting president withdrew his candidacy to seek a second term and endorsed his vice president.

---

4. Bible Hub, "Guard Against."

Introduction

Several close colleagues called for President Joseph Biden to step down, reportedly due to concerns about his failing health. He felt he would step down if he thought his health would be a determinant to his country, which he loved, or if the polling numbers showed that he needed a clear path to winning the election. On Sunday, July 21, 2024, President Joseph Biden announced that he would not seek a second term and endorsed Vice President Kamala Harris as his successor to the presidency of the United States. Within twenty-four hours, she and her supporters reportedly raised $81 million—an unprecedented amount—and secured the support of governors, senators, representatives, unions, and other key stakeholders. Significantly, the money raised was from first-time donors who believed in her candidacy.

A Zoom call hosted by the Win with Black Women, founded by Jataka Eaddy, reportedly connected with 44,000 women and raised $1.2 million for the Harris campaign in just three hours. On Monday, July 22, 2024, 20,000 Black men participated in a Zoom call and reportedly raised $1.5 million. In addition, White sisters and brothers also raised millions of dollars in support of the Harris campaign. This demonstrated that we could organize, and with our hand in God's, we know all things are possible. It was a historic moment. This unification demonstrated what we can achieve when we unite for a common cause, even when it may negatively impact people's lives and alter our country and democracy as we know them. It showed what the consequences of obedience and unification bring when we listen to the still, small voice of the Holy Spirit and follow instructions. The people heard, listened, and followed directions that led to changes in their life circumstances. Because of the ability to listen, work together, and obey God, White sisters and brothers heard and observed our cry and, for the sake of our democracy, joined the common cause that would impact all people, the nation, and the world.

President Joe Biden's endorsement of Vice President Kamala Harris ignited the country like a wildfire in an arid western desert or a deluge of water pushing its way through a valley; the surge had unbelievable force, and united people with a common cause.

Accessorization

Regardless of age, economic and social status, educational background, community orientation, faith, and belief, people united to defeat MAGA (Make America Great Again), bringing a sense of security to some and to our democracy. Who said it could not be done? Who said Black people were not smart enough to organize and gain strength through and from all people interested in a democracy, and perceived as a severe threat to what we enjoy and have experienced? God knows how to allow a threat to fester in a country and bring people together on one accord. This was a historic movement of epic proportions.

Do we recognize a need to change our accessories as a nation and a people? Are our lifestyles, thoughts, and perspectives aligned with God's expectations? Have we allowed ourselves to become so entrenched in AI, power, and control that we are losing our way in the bleakness of the dark abyss? Are our relationship and bonds established, and are they no longer cemented and sealed in our faith? As we stand in the shadows of life's journey, looking to see a bright beam pointing us to a changing world filled with AI, hate, frustration, deaths, and bigotry directing, leading, threatening, and controlling people's paths, we wonder what lies ahead. The mist has become so thick that we can barely see our fingers as we reach through, trying to grasp something that gives us hope, stability, and a desire to pull ourselves over to the other side. We see a vague reflection of what was. We allowed ourselves to be encamped by the accessories of control, hate, jealousy, anger, a need for power, retaliation, and getting even with people. In some instances, we have become avengers, covetous, envious, and gossipers. The other person cannot be you, and you fear they want to take you down and destroy what you have accomplished. The apostle Paul provides us with an array of emotional feelings outlined in Gal 5:17, just before he presents the construct Jesus gives us in Gal 5:22–23—a road map to righteousness and a Spirit-filled lifestyle. There was an election, but it didn't turn out as millions had thought. There is still some questioning about the Electoral College results. One can only say, "How fascinating." Only God knows the rationale for the results, and only God knows what lies ahead.

1

Consequences for Disobedience
Life-Altering

The prospect of the righteous is joy, but the hopes of the wicked come to nothing.

Prov 10:28

Because you have rejected the Lord's word, he has rejected you as king.

1 Sam 15:23

THE ABOVE PASSAGE IN Proverbs is a key Scripture that addresses disobedience and its consequences. A similar passage is found in 1 Samuel. This Scripture in 1 Samuel lays out the life-altering consequences for disobeying God and the serious consequences of rejecting his word. Therefore, disobedience is as much a sin as divination, and stubbornness is as bad as idolatry. If you do not live up to God's expectations for obedience, you are seen as rebellious, rejecting his authority, challenging his sovereignty, and

Accessorization

refusing to follow his commands. A significant consequence for not following God's expectation is spending eternity in hell if you do not seek repentance for your disobedient actions. From a biblical perspective, expectation refers to an anticipated act. According to the *Collins English Dictionary*, expectation is the act or the state of expecting to wait in expectation."[1]

God set his expectations for humanity in the garden of Eden by forming man in his image from the dust of the earth and breathing the breath of life into him. Subsequently, the woman was created by removing a rib from the man's side. God gave Adam precise and distinct instructions for his expectations in the garden and the consequences of disobedience. He gave Adam a whole realm of trees to eat from, except the tree of knowledge in the middle of the garden, and disobeying God's instructions would result in death, not a physical death but a spiritual death, a disconnect and break of *koinonia* (a Greek word which signifies Christian fellowship, communion, or sharing in common)[2] from God. This consequence may be documented as man's first lesson in obedience, following instructions, and learning the consequences for his actions when he disobeyed God's command. The Old Testament book of Proverbs 4:1–27 (NIV) enumerates what you are expected to do, especially when it comes to wisdom, including learning good judgment, gaining understanding, following God's command, listening, paying attention, and living by these expectations. However, you must cultivate wisdom and godliness, and make informed decisions based on these principles. As believers, the writer advises you not to turn your back on wisdom (the Hebrew word for wisdom, "*chokhmah*," is grammatically feminine), because she will protect you. He further encourages you to love wisdom, as she will guard you, and, above all, he says you should prize wisdom, for she will make you great. There is, however, a responsibility on your part, the believer, and that is obedience and adherence to God's word. This brings you to the context of Solomon, the wisest man who ever lived. His wisdom was displayed

---

1. *Collins Dictionary*, "Expectation."
2. Vine et al., *Expository Dictionary*, 90.

Consequences for Disobedience

when two women were fighting over the same baby; one woman's baby died during the night, and she took the other woman's baby. Rather than dealing with a hearing or a court of their peers, Solomon ordered his soldiers to cut the baby in half—he knew that the birth mother would instead give the baby up and let it live instead of killing the child and dividing it in half to each woman. The birth mother cried out to let the woman have the child. Throughout the New Testament, Jesus provides guidelines and expectations through parables and teachings, using examples to help you understand their biblical meaning. However, disobeying God's expectations and instructions is not a new phenomenon. He divinely laid out his expectations for you to follow, enabling you to steer clear of life's pitfalls and temptations. These instructions began with the first command given to man in the garden of Eden. However, due to imperfections and selectivity in hearing, man broke his relationship, fellowship, and oneness with God. In the garden of Eden, he gave Adam and Eve clear instructions about his expectations of them. If Adam had followed them, you would have an abundant life free of worry, trials, tribulations, pain, and suffering. You, however, know what happened when Eve allowed herself to be tricked by the serpent's cunning voice and participated in a theological conversation with him.

God expected Adam and Eve, whom he created in a state of innocence, in the image of God and in perfect harmony, to be obedient and follow his instructions given explicitly to Adam in Gen 2:16–17 (KJV). God commanded that Adam could eat freely of every tree in the garden except the tree of "knowledge of good and evil, thou shalt not eat of it: for in the day that thou eatest thereof thou shalt surely die." Scripture speaks of three deaths: a physical death, which is separation of the body and spirit; spiritual death, separation of the individual from God; and eternal death, the final state of the lost person in the "lake of fire," termed the "second death." This is separation from God forever (Rev 20:10, 14 KJV). The book of Genesis, written by Moses, tells you how God, in his infinite wisdom, created man from the dust of the earth for his glory, and he named man "Adam." He placed him amid the

Accessorization

garden east of Eden, along with his wife, Eve, to enjoy the eternal fruits of God's creation. He blessed man with the capacity of eternal life, perfect and precious in God's sight, and he gave man dominion over every living creature and fruit that had seed. What a gracious favor for man to have been afforded this privilege, blessing, and opportunity to be over such splendor. One of his primary tasks was to name each creature in the garden. In addition, God expected Adam to be obedient and fruitful, to replenish and subdue the earth, and to maintain what God had provided. God gave them his generous permission to eat freely of all the trees in the garden except the tree of the knowledge of good and evil, and he gave them the consequences for disobedience and self-will.

It is difficult to determine when the serpent used God's words surreptitiously to influence Eve and Adam's thinking. His cunning made them forget the abundance of God's love and favor, the gift of eternal life, the great fertility, the splendor, and the enjoyment of all that was created. Most importantly, Scripture does not give you a time when they forgot about God's command and the consequences they would suffer for their actions during this conversation with the serpent.

This act may have occurred over a period of time or shortly after its creation. There is no evidence of the period, but it happened. Adam and Eve had the opportunity to explore the garden that God created. Imagine that Eve may have become bored with their routine over some time. The tree's fruit intensified Eve's curiosity amid the garden, and combined with her human desire, temptation, and the serpent's strategy, she began to question why not that particular tree? Why had God commanded Adam not to eat or touch the tree, and if they did, the consequences would be death? How often had Eve stood before the tree and coveted its fruit, and how often did the serpent observe her behavior? Perhaps with the "what if?" What could happen to her if she took one bite of the fruit? How often do you, as believers, fail to see that it is not the magnitude of the sin but the sin itself and its subsequent consequences? You may think of the temptation's immediacy rather than its consequences. Like Eve, you move forward and sometimes invite others to join you because you don't want to be alone in your mess. You may tell your friends some half-truths to pull them into your mess and hook them. You know you cannot afford that new car with all its unique amenities or that new house in a particular gated community, but after thinking and dreaming about it, like Eve, you move forward. Scripture does not tell you if this was Eve's first time admiring the tree or the first time the serpent approached, tempted, and appealed to her covetous ego. The serpent, however, put forth a theological challenge that she could no longer resist. She blocked out God's command and listened to the serpent's cunning rhetoric. Perhaps he caught Eve at a vulnerable moment, as he may have caught some of you by surprise when you were at your lowest point, and he plays on your vulnerability, allowing you to be taken in by his suggestions. His conversation with Eve may have proceeded: "Now Eve, you and Adam have lived in delight in this garden eastward in Eden since God created you. You enjoyed all of the beautiful things here, including the fruits of the trees and vines. Why do you think your God does not want you to eat the fruit of that tree amid the garden, Eve? Now, don't you find it odd? What about that tree that your God does not want you to experience? Think about it, Eve. Look at that tree, Eve, with its magnificent and angelic beauty. It is the tallest and greenest amid the garden. Its shiny and symmetrically shaped fruit appears more delicious than any other you and Adam have tasted, wouldn't you say? It is a beauty to behold. I would suspect, Eve, your God is a bit selfish and wants to keep this knowledge and the secrets of the fruit for himself. Don't you think it is rather odd, Eve?" Isn't this how you are approached with a comparative and questioning analysis that raises doubt about an issue you have some truth about? You convince yourself that it is all right because you want to engage, but you must first accessorize the situation to make it better than it truly is. How often have you had a similar conversation?

 The serpent questions Eve as to what God told her the fruit represented. She repeated, "The fruit of the tree represents the knowledge of good and evil and is designed to make one wise." By averting God's exact words, Eve got into a theological conversation

Accessorization

with the serpent. Ah! He continues, "So, your God told you to eat freely of the fruit of any tree in the garden. But of the fruit of the tree amid the garden, your God has commanded that you do not eat of it, or you shall surely die." The serpent's smooth demeanor and compassion in his voice convinced Eve that they would not die. He inquired about Eve's ability to serve a God who did not reveal the truth to them.

The serpent was amazed that God restricted Adam and Eve from freely choosing any fruit in the garden. He focused on God's restrictive command of the fruit and began by placing doubt in Eve's heart about God's word. He persuaded her to believe that God had said they could eat freely from every fruit in the garden. Carelessly, by free will or ego, Eve convinced herself that the serpent's interpretation was correct. She purposely exaggerated the limitations God had given them, thereby minimizing their punishment of death. She told the serpent of the subsequent death they would suffer at the hands of God if they ate the fruit. The serpent continued to appeal to Eve's ego through his cunning and jovial nature. He took Eve's attention away from God's goodness, favor, and all the provisions he made for them in the garden. He was able to focus her attention on the forbidden fruit, suggesting again that God was withholding something from them. This doubt-casting against God's word happens so frequently with you. You sometimes cannot appreciate what God has blessed you with, allowing self-doubt and self-will to cast doubt on what God has said and moving outside of his will, provision, power, and protection, similar to Adam and Eve. It is possible that the serpent played with Eve's mind and emotions, convincing her that by eating the forbidden fruit, the consequences would not be death, but gaining knowledge, power, and equality with God. The serpent may have convinced her that God told them they would die to frighten and keep them submissive to his will. He may have encouraged her to eat the fruit and enjoy the challenge, but God's warning prevented them from experiencing it. After all, God created them in his image, and why would he then allow them to die? Does that sound like a just God, Eve? The serpent may have continued, "But

Consequences for Disobedience

I promise you that once you taste how delicious the fruit is, you will wonder why you did not try it sooner than today. Oh, and Eve, don't forget to share a piece with Adam; you will have experiences and joy beyond your wildest dreams." Eve failed to understand that the death she would experience was not physical but spiritual, a break in oneness and fellowship with God that she had experienced since their creation. The serpent knew this but did not share this information with Eve.

There are many cunning, deceptive, and disingenuous serpents in your life, convincing and encouraging you to move against the will of God. You often have blessings in your hands, and sometimes, like Adam and Eve, you sacrifice those blessings for what you perceive to be a faster and greater reward. Adam and Eve had everything anyone could hope for or dream of in humanity. They had God's abundant and unmerited grace, mercy, blessings, favor, fellowship, and divine sanction. God gave them everything except permission to eat or touch the fruit of the tree amid the garden. How often does God direct you to the right path, yet you choose another because of optical illusion, false perceptions, or sometimes due simply to greed? How frequently do you know the restrictions and perhaps may have some idea of the life-altering consequences, yet you sacrifice what you have for immediate gratification or personal gain? How frequently do you forget moral discernment? How often has the serpent tempted you, and you convince yourself that it is OK because a good, understanding God would not deny you specific things?

The serpent finally convinced Eve that if she and Adam ate the fruit from the forbidden tree, he guaranteed they would not die. Instead, their eyes would be opened, and they would become like "gods," knowing good and evil. Eve did eat the fruit and gave a portion to her husband as the serpent had instructed. This act of disobedience to God's command and their decision to follow the serpent's words caused them to fall into sin, bringing the curse of sin on the entire human race and God's creation for all generations. Before eating the fruit, they had integrity and walked naked daily. They were not ashamed because of their innocence of sin, purity of thought, and moral nature. They could walk among the wild beasts and other dangerous animals without fear.

Because disobedience and the inability to resist temptation or the whisper of "you will not die" resonated with Eve's curiosity, she followed the serpent's instructions, consumed a portion of the fruit, and shared the rest with Adam. Following this act of disobedience and stepping outside God's expectations, their eyes were opened to see everything due to their sinfulness; this was a life-altering consequence. They realized they were naked and felt a sense of guilt and shame before each other and before God. Because of this realization, they did not want to face him. Adam knew he had not done what was expected of him. He had doubted God's word and accepted the word of his wife, who had allowed herself to be tricked by the serpent. Adam probably wondered how he could have allowed his heart to be deceived. He may have thought about what he had done. Why did he believe the woman? He probably felt despair, fear, hopelessness, and loneliness. A barrier now existed between him and God. He no longer experienced a close, intimate relationship with God and probably felt as some children feel when they disobey their parents. God called him, just like a loving parent, perhaps annoyed when the child disobeyed, and the punishment had severe consequences. God knew he must carry out the punishment and was pained by its outcome. Adam may have wondered if an act of disobedience would end his life here in Eden as he reflected on what God had initially told him. If he ate from that particular tree, he would surely die. He probably began to wonder about the fate he would face when God passed final judgment on him. He finally answered God, who asked him what he had done. "Why Adam? Why did you disobey me?" Of course, like many of you, Adam played the blame game (Gen 3:12). God was furious. There was a severe price to pay for their disobedience.

Adam and Eve, like children caught with their hands in the cookie jar, immediately looked for a covering to hide their naked bodies before God. When God asked why they had eaten the fruit, Adam, like so many individuals today, did not accept responsibility for his actions. He immediately blamed Eve and attempted to

Consequences for Disobedience

deflect his failure onto God by blaming the woman God gave him. In essence, he was also pointing the finger at God, and if God had not given him that woman who encouraged him to eat from the forbidden tree, none of this would have happened. Adam trusted Eve and thought she had his best interests and concerns at heart. After all, he told God, "You gave the woman to me for a helpmate," and now she tempted him and caused him to sin, and now he was being punished for disobeying God's command. Adam failed to understand and accept the responsibility God gave him before Eve's creation, including the command and its consequences. God expected him to follow the instructions laid out for them in Gen 2:16–17. And the Lord commanded the man, "You are free to eat from any tree in the garden, but you must not eat from the tree of the knowledge of good and evil, for when you eat of it, you will surely die."

Like many of you, Eve immediately blamed the serpent for tempting her to eat the fruit rather than taking responsibility for her curiosity, egotistical needs, lustful and covetous nature, actions, and self-directedness. Each player began to blame the other, an evasive tactic they used to cast suspicion. We hear evasive excuses all too often, and no one is willing to accept responsibility: "I thought," "I didn't know," "I didn't believe this would happen," "It's his fault," "He made me do it." It is heartbreaking when you do not accept responsibility for your actions or the life-altering consequences of your disobedience. You often confuse your reality and place yourself in circumstances that lead you to justify what seems like reasonable evil and wrongdoing. God was furious and disappointed that Adam did not follow his command. It must have pained God to expel his creation from the garden as punishment for their disobedience. He placed an eternal curse on each of the parties involved, and no one was exempt from punishment. The serpent, who walked upright and talked, was cursed to crawl on his belly through eternity and was doomed to eat dust all the days of his life. What a substantial life-altering sacrifice and punishment the serpent suffered for encouraging disobedience to God's command and placing an obstacle in man's path that has eternal

Accessorization

repercussions. Did the serpent not know that God was aware of his conversation with Eve and that his actions would have severe consequences, affecting his position in Eden and his eternal fate? Was he under the impression that God would not punish him for his role in the fall of man? Did he not understand God's omniscience, omnipotence, and omnipresence? This is so relevant in today's society. The man continues to sin, and this does not please God. Man's behavior of hiding and doing things during the night is relevant to Adam and Eve's behavior when they tried to hide their nakedness from God. However, you do not appear to have the same level of embarrassment today as they had in the garden. You commit and display all kinds of jealous behavior; you lie, steal, cheat, and bear false witnesses, and the list is endless. However, God continues to give cues and clues about his expectations, yet people fail to grasp or heed them.

Following their disobedience, God gave each participant the severity of their punishment for their disobedient behavior. Consequently, God cursed the ground he gave Adam and told him in Gen 3:18-19 (NIV), "It will produce thorns and thistles for you. . . . By the sweat of your brow, you will eat your food until you return to the ground." Man would work hard and labor for his livelihood. Because of Eve's disobedience, she and all women would go through the pain associated with childbearing. From a personal perspective, I cannot tell you I understand the pain women experience during childbirth, as I was not blessed with the privilege of being a natural mom. Still, I am a stepmom and mother to many. This same proclamation made by God in Genesis is also noted in Isa 26:17: "A woman with child and about to give birth writhes and cries out in her pain, so were we in your presence, O Lord." God gave Adam specific instructions and expected him to follow through by being obedient. In some respects, you are like your brother Adam, blaming others for his shortcomings. Imagine God's disappointment with Adam, whom he created in his own image. God commanded him not to eat the fruit of the tree in the middle of the garden. Imagine how it must have felt for a father to impose such a harsh punishment on his son when he

Consequences for Disobedience

had to expel him from Eden and place angels at the gate to prevent his reentry. It must have been tough for God, the man he created with love and in great detail, to blow the breath of life into him to make him a living soul, and now he, like a mom, must administer everlasting punishment.

The fruit has eternal life-altering consequences for you. God judged them according to his will for their sin and disobedience. The expulsion was more than a physical move; it was a fall from grace, a spiritual separation, and a spiritual death for man. God knew that Adam had no experience with good and evil, but through God's love and compassion (mercy), he endowed man with grace and redemption through the Adamic covenant. God put enmity between the serpent and the woman and placed a spiritual barrier between the serpent's and the woman's seed. He expelled them from the garden and made it impossible for them to reenter. The blame game, you could say, was birthed in the garden. Deception, you may say, was birthed in the garden of Eden, and indeed, sin was born. Each participant pointed the finger at the next; neither was willing to accept responsibility for their action of self-will, self-determination, self-direction, and self-absorption. Each had self-will and did not need to participate in the scheme conjured by the serpent, which had life-altering consequences and lasting implications.

Imagine what it must have felt like when they were forced to spend their first night outside Eden without the presence and voice of God, with whom they had communed since creation. Can you feel Adam's fear and frustration in finding food and shelter? Everything was at his fingertips in Eden: food was plenteous, and now, they needed to fend for themselves. They required clothing other than the fig leaves they wore in Eden immediately following their sin. Adam probably experienced pain for the first time and learned what it felt like to kill for the first time. Ah! However, this is not the end of mankind; a gracious and just God gave man another opportunity through the birth, teachings, humble and compassionate life, death, and resurrection of his Son, Jesus, who allowed himself to suffer humiliation, carry a cross laden with

Accessorization

the sin of man; he allowed himself to be crucified on an old, rugged cross with spikes in his feet, nails in his hands, a crown of thorns pushed into his head, pierced in his side, until blood and water came streaming down from his body; he was buried in a borrowed tomb. Three days later, he was resurrected on Sunday morning. His death bore your sins, past, present, and future. All you must do is live as God has commanded, love one another, and love God. This seems so simplistic. Yet, it is the most challenging task to love everybody. This means you must humble yourself, be submissive to God, and learn to make appropriate choices through the exercise of your free will. Adam and Eve's faith in God's will and instructions was evaluated. If they had not been clear about his instructions, they could have sought further clarification of the phrase "You will surely die." Instead, they allowed the serpent to cloud their thinking, placing doubt in their hearts and leading them to take the forbidden fruit.

You must follow the perfect instructions from Jesus to add valuable accessories, such as faith, replacing fear with trust, forgiving others as God forgives you, believing in the power and source of God, and seeking repentance and following Jesus, your Savior and Redeemer. You must also become more versatile by seeking a deeper understanding of God's will and plan for your life, aligning your life's goals, and growing in wisdom and knowledge through studying his word. What does it take to be an obedient child of God? It takes a lifestyle change, putting off the old self and putting on the new one, which has been immersed in the pool of forgiveness, washed in the blood of the Lamb, and sprouting up a new creature ready and willing to follow God's word, instructions, and expectations. To better understand the life-altering consequences of disobedience, I refer you to the twenty-eighth chapter of the book of Deuteronomy, specifically the "curses for disobedience" in the NIV.

2

Accessorizing Your Christian Character and Self-Absorbed Nature (Temperament) in the Body of Christ

> *Let the word of Christ dwell in you richly in all wisdom; teaching and admonishing one another in psalms and hymns and spiritual songs, singing with grace in your hearts to the Lord. And whatsoever ye do in word or deed, do all in the name of the Lord Jesus, giving thanks to God and the Father by him.*
> Col 3:16–17 KJV

ACCESSORIZING SOMETHING, SUCH AS furniture, clothing, or certain foods, adds other things (like grilled broccoli, lemon, or asparagus) to make it look more attractive. In fashion, accessories enhance or complement an item, thereby contributing to the overall appeal of the outfit and making it more appealing to buyers. Accessorization, which first appeared in 1935 as a new English word, is the process of accessorizing oneself with additional attractions or personal adornment. Accessorization is about complementing,

Accessorization

embellishing, and making something more visually interesting or personal, whether in fashion or interior design. It also assists one in expressing their identity and personality.[1] Some individuals seem self-absorbed when it comes to accessorizing. According to the *Oxford Languages Dictionary*, self-absorption is a preoccupation with one's own emotions, interests, or situations, or being overly concerned with oneself, including feelings and thoughts.[2] These terminologies concern your feelings, behavior, identity, and outer appearance.

Accessorization can change your appearance at a moment's notice, making a statement that reflects your personality, inspires your inner being, and gives you that "I got it" fashion statement. Accessories, such as the basic suit or evening dress, pulled together with the right complements, give you a sophisticated, well-balanced appearance. You, however, know how difficult it is to change ingrained attitudes, which are feelings or opinions about something or someone, or a way of behaving. It is often difficult to change attitudes and beliefs. It will take time. And time means you must learn to wait. Learning to wait is a crucial aspect of spiritual growth, as it fosters patience and trust in God's plan. As Isa 40:27–31 tells you, God expects you to learn to wait. Several scenarios demonstrate how waiting can be beneficial and help you grow in patience as you learn to hope and trust in God. When you drape yourself in God's delight, learn to have faith in him, in his word, and obey him, you will receive favor and blessings from him. However, remember that your belief and faith do not guarantee you will not experience disappointments, challenges, opposition, and trials. These life accessories are genuine and seem to lead you away from the righteous path you have chosen. These detours sometimes present themselves as doubts, questions, and fears, temporarily blinding you and shaking your very core, your faith. It is only a test to check the depth of your faith. Remember what God did for you in the past and how he brought you through great trials and tribulations, because you can take everything to

1. *Oxford Learner's Dictionaries*, "Accessorize."
2. *Oxford Learner's Dictionaries*, "Self-Absorption."

Accessorizing Your Christian Character and Self-Absorbed Nature

God in prayer. You find abundant joy, hope, and peace in knowing that the Holy Spirit indwells you, as a believer, and serves as a wall between you and Satan's stronghold. God intercedes, and there is evidence of change. The tongue that speaks ill will, the anger portrayed by the driver, the lie told by a coworker or friend, and the frustration displayed are all dissipated by change agents for Christ. The promise of enmity made to man by God in the garden of Eden is illustrated to you through the birth of Jesus to a virgin in a stable. It is evident that God loves you and has compassion for you by sacrificing his only Son for your salvation. God expects you to keep your temple (body) pure and accessorize it with prayers, praise, meditation, and his holy word. I urge believers not to become entangled and snared in Satan's trap, but to accessorize their lives with the word of God, to walk with the Spirit of God, who will help them walk with God and stay in his will and his way through obedience. God expects you not to harbor evil thoughts toward one another. He desires you to be Christlike. This is sometimes easier said than practiced. Your fleshly selves get in the way, and you allow yourselves to think of getting even with that particular person, inflicting pain on them, setting up curves and snares on life's journey to slow them down.

The book of Esther clearly illustrates what happens when you attempt to dig a hole or set up detours for another believer. You must not allow your anger, jealousy, and need to cause harm to another individual because you are afraid of losing position, power, and public recognition to them. I admonish you to think about Haman, and his plot against the Jews. King Xerxes appointed him over all the nobles, elevating him to the most powerful office in the empire. This is like many believers; give them a title and a position, and it goes straight to their heads. They immediately assume authority without regard for or appreciation of God. They assume a vengeful role, using their position for the wrong purpose. Read the third chapter of Esther, and note how Haman, after receiving King Xerxes's signet ring, was told to do with the Jews as he pleased. His first misguided will, led by greed and hatred, was to eliminate Esther and her people. She, however, had gained favor with the

Accessorization

king and requested to present her petition to him, but only after the banquet she planned for him and Haman (Esth 6:7). Mordecai was present at the banquet. Imagine Haman's anger, inner rage, and fury when he observed Mordecai's presence; this sent Haman off the deep end. He restrained his emotions and went home to his wife and friends, who, rather than encouraging him to accept what is, encouraged him to build a gallows with precise measurements to hang Mordecai. However, as divine providence would have it, Mordecai uncovered a conspiracy to assassinate the king and shared the information with King Xerxes. The king asked Haman a question that met his greedy appetite. What honors could he bestow upon a faithful servant? Haman presented the king with a litany of honors, thinking it was himself the king was referring to. In short, Haman was removed from the palace and hanged on the gallows he had built for Mordecai. You must be very careful when digging a ditch for someone, as you might end up falling in it yourself. Haman did not expect to die; he had planned everything out to meet Mordecai and Esther's demise. Mordecai, the Jew, was highly esteemed because he worked for the good of his people and advocated for their welfare. Vengeance is mine, said the Lord. Remember God's words, instructions, and expectations for you as believers; and remember, only God avenges.

When contemplating accessorization, remember that you are told to do everything in love (1 Cor 16:13). Be on guard, stand firm in the faith, be men of courage, be strong, and understand that you must and may be alone in and with the Lord. Accessorize yourself with the perfect instructions from Jesus to add valuable accessories, such as faith, humility, replacing fear with trust, believing in the power and source of God, walking in the Spirit, and following Jesus as your Savior and Redeemer. Believers are becoming more versatile in their walk by seeking a deeper understanding of God and his formidable power, extending love to his children, and gaining a greater knowledge of what God expects of them as believers and followers of his word. You must continue to accessorize your lives by growing in his grace, wisdom, and understanding; by

Accessorizing Your Christian Character and Self-Absorbed Nature

studying his words and developing an intimate relationship with him.

As believers, you face daily challenges and tests of your faith, and sometimes, life circumstances can be overwhelming. You are often confronted and cast down by a reverberating tongue that boasts and changes life's trajectory. You must be careful how you allow words to spew from your tongue with an awareness of the danger these words can cause. Coupled with the tongue is the internal spiritual barometer that life's challenges can easily tap. Suppose you are not careful and not spiritually built up! In that case, you may find yourself in a terrific situation, and due to the explosive surroundings, the problem can ignite like a forest fire, consuming everything in its path. You may find yourself losing control; however, allowing the Lord to be in charge is different from losing control out of fear of not being in charge. You must accessorize each circumstance with prayer, asking God to continue to cover you and direct your path as you face these situations daily. However, you must guard your spirit and not allow Satan to cause you to lose control. You do not know who is watching to witness how you manage stress, negative attitudes, or behavior towards you. You must always be vigilant and on guard. Sin is always lurking to cause you to fall and lose control of your Christian values and spirituality. Guarding against negative influences, whether virtual, in person, or through the general mail, is crucial to maintaining a Christlike character.

You must learn to adorn yourself with the supernatural graces of spiritual gifts given to believers by God through the Holy Spirit to build up the body of Christ. Additionally, you must embrace the characteristics of the fruit of the Spirit and remember that the Holy Spirit dwells within you. God has provided you with these gifts not to benefit yourselves as believers but to glorify him as your Lord and Savior. These gifts are intended to build up his church further, helping you become better witnesses in your mission "to go," making disciples, enlightening, encouraging, and assisting the body of Christ to grow spiritually and become more like him. Through the gifts of grace, you are armed with incredible knowledge about the impact of disobedience on the brokenness and dysfunction in

Accessorization

your community, encompassing individuals, families, churches, schools, and businesses. It is time for you to take a closer look at a world based on a conceptual plan similar to what Nehemiah introduced to his people. Some of these strategies may be relevant to the blight, bleakness, and brokenness you experience in your community or perhaps in your home. A resurgence of evil in your surroundings exacerbates many critical issues. How do you fight this growing monster? With the word of God immersed in his perfect plan for his children. How do you stand under the heavy burden and weight of continuing lies, deception, retributive language, and a willingness to lay a crooked path for others to attempt to cross? How do you instill courage and resurge faith and hope in a world where there is so much deceit and cunning talk that the spirit of man is dying right before your eyes? Untruths, half-truths, and falsehoods are being disseminated in an attempt to overshadow truth and the word of God. You have been given God's Spirit, and you therefore know the truth. You see the difference between right and wrong. The writing of 1 John 3 (attributed to John the apostle) identifies a liar as "anyone who says that Jesus is not the Christ." However, anyone who acknowledges the Son as the Father speaks truth (1 John 3:20–23 NLT). It does not matter what the course; as believers, you must remain faithful to the things you have been taught. You are encouraged to continue in fellowship and oneness in God. It may seem difficult and perhaps confusing at times, overwhelming, and even unfair, but persevere, remain the course, and be the victor; you will enjoy eternal life as promised by God.

How can you encourage a man who believes he is in power and has control over another when his feet steadily sank from under him? How can you help people see that only God, the Author, Creator, Finisher, and Holder of the universe, is in control? By his majestic power, people will live by God's design or die believing they are in control. As you ponder, turn to the first chapter of Revelation; God tells you, "'I am the Alpha and the Omega—the beginning and the end,' says the Lord God. 'I am the one who is, who always was, and who is still to come—the Almighty One'" (Rev 1:8 NLT).

Accessorizing Your Christian Character and Self-Absorbed Nature

1. The Tongue: Small and Dangerous

Even so, the tongue is a little member, and boasteth great things. Behold, how great a matter a little fire kindleth! And the tongue is a fire, a world of iniquity: so is the tongue among our members, that it defileth the whole body, and setteth on fire the course of nature; and it is set on fire of hell. . . . But the tongue can no man tame; it is an unruly evil, full of deadly poison.

Jas 3:5–6, 8 KJV

A gentle answer turns away wrath, but a harsh word stirs up anger. The tongue of the wise commends knowledge, but the mouth of the fool gushes folly. . . . The tongue that brings healing is a tree of life, but a deceitful tongue crushes the spirit.

Prov 15:1–2, 4 NIV

The tongue is a free fire; if you are not careful, it will corrupt and consume the whole body. It is similar to a match, with a tiny head filled with sulfur at the end. When a match is struck carelessly against a suitable surface with the right strength, it can ignite a forest and destroy delicate plants and creatures. Like the match, you must guard your tongue and be gentle with your words that may come forth and burn the very emotional self of another individual. When you have a free moment, analyze your language; you may gain a better understanding of the power of your tongue. In Col 3:7–10, you are instructed to walk in the life you once lived in these ways. However, you must now rid yourselves of all such things as anger, rage, malice, slander, gossip, and filthy language from your lips, or, better yet, spend some time with Paul. He tells you that you must not lie to each other since you have taken off your old self with its practices and have put on the new self, which is being renewed in knowledge in the image of the Creator. As believers, you have the word of God bound in your heart, and thus, because of this close bond with the Lord, your speech and most definitely your tongue are seasoned with the salt Paul talks

Accessorization

about in Col 4:6, where he states, "Let your conversation be always full of grace, seasoned with salt, so that you may know how to answer everyone." You must remember that the words you speak, the behavior you portray, or the temperament you display must represent your Lord and Savior's goodness towards you. Otherwise, your public image or private conduct may be offensive to others and, most importantly, God. It challenges you to take the saltshaker and turn it upside down while holding it in your hand. Observe the salt flowing from the shaker as it falls in any direction, hitting anything in its path. Each grain represents words spurred from your tongue, hitting and hurting anything in their path. How can blessings, honor, and praise to God come from the same tongue that curses a brother or sister? This is inconsistent thinking. You must be reminded that the things that come out of your attitude, your behavior, your thoughts, and your actions reveal what is truly inside of you; what is truly in the content of your heart will work its way to the tip of your tongue and find its way to others negatively or painfully. How do you curb your tongue amid anger and lies that consistently destroy your person and integrity? Human nature is often too offensive to protect you from the immediate embarrassment and pain that can suddenly hit you. The onset of pain is immediate, and your reaction may often be anger, expressed through harsher language. This behavior occurs when you respond without thinking or praying to seek God's guidance through the Holy Spirit. However, if you stop, think, and listen to the essence of their words, you can hear anger, feel emotional pain and stress, and become defensive, preparing to strike before the other person reacts. The other person has made you the object of their issues and has now scapegoated you into an emotional roller coaster. The scapegoating process is sometimes used because the other person feels safe putting you in that position, because they may recognize the Christ in you. However, God continues to accessorize his believers by allowing the Holy Spirit to indwell within you and shield you through this brief period of pain, emotional suffering, and darkness. He hears your pains, groans, frustrations, and anger and intercedes on your behalf.

Accessorizing Your Christian Character and Self-Absorbed Nature

As believers, your walk and talk may be an excellent opportunity for you to help others. You must let your behavior be such that you use every opportunity to witness the Lord. You must evangelize the goodness of his favor and his loving compassion. You don't need to carry an enormous Bible or wear the most significant gold cross to let others know you are a disciple of Christ. As disciples, your behavior, manners, and attitudes are accessories reflecting who you are and whom you serve. Be that beacon of light that shines in the darkness, showing others the way, the way to salvation.

Jesus is the light of the world. As dark and difficult periods and issues impact lives, as you recently experienced during the 2024 presidential election, remember the green pasture God has prepared for you, as written in Ps 23—a pasture where you can graze and dwell as long as necessary. You can stream a picture of the pasture in your mind and focus on where the Shepherd abides, allowing you to come amid the darkness that shrouds and troubles your soul. But he knows that when you gaze upon the pasture by the quiet stream, flowing gently through the ruggedness of life, you regain your composure and are engulfed by a peaceful spirit that brings calmness, a place without thirst, hunger, hate, confusion, or judgment. You can reflect on the great table he has prepared for you in the presence of your enemies, and then he promises to anoint your head with oil; your cup will run over because you have been so blessed with goodness and mercy. God lets you know he is there, and your great Shepherd, with his staff stretched forth to guide you to him, lets you know, "I got you, my child." Just as he parted the waters and allowed his children, the Israelites, to cross over on dry land, he can do the same for you in this twenty-first century with its virtual hatreds. So, you must continue to let your life shine and see the goodness in others. As believers, your walk may be an excellent opportunity to help someone. Let your behavior be so displayed that you use every opportunity to witness the Lord. To evangelize the goodness of the Lord, you don't always need to carry your Bible with you at all times. Remember to keep

Accessorization

your attitude accessorized to help you remember God's expectations for obedience.

Strive to keep your tongue from spewing out words and information like an erupting volcano, where ash, rocks, boulders, and fire come forth simultaneously and rush down the mountainside, burning and destroying everything in their path. Spewing words from your tongue can cause similar damage and is not part of Christ. Just as the volcanic eruption destroys, so do your words, cutting deeply and painfully, leaving invisible scars that may never heal. While you may apologize and try to soothe and rebuild relationships, like the forest after a fire, it takes time. In some instances, new shoots may never mature. Saying "I am sorry" may make the perpetrator feel better, but it may also be a form of self-aggrandizing. The pain, suffering, and humiliation experienced by the victim cannot be recalled or erased; those words spewed out in anger or jealousy are like the wind blowing through on its way and cannot be reclaimed. The believer has allowed Satan to cause them to destroy another person. You permit Satan to rage storms in your life, to distract and destroy you from doing what is right and holy in the sight of God. Knowing the dangers and storms the tongue can initiate and the raging fire it is capable of, you must be careful to keep Christ in your midst. You should pray, stop, wait, cry, and think before acting. It is not easy, but through and with Christ, it is possible. Just seek.

Scenario 1

I was at a bank, patiently waiting in line to be served. The person in front of me had allowed himself to become agitated by the wait and the initial issue that had brought him to the bank. As he approached the window, his anger spread throughout the bank; we all felt his accusatory and demeaning nature, along with the discussion of his business issue. I sensed that the other customers were experiencing the same emotions I was. We were embarrassed for the person who had initially assisted him but had not completed the transaction as he had anticipated or assumed it would. We glanced at each other, hoping the customer would calm down

Accessorizing Your Christian Character and Self-Absorbed Nature

and accept the assistance being provided. We lowered our heads and looked at, and sometimes over, another person, just wanting him to lower his tone. Finally, one of the managers came over to distract him; it was apparent that his conversation with her was his sign of escape. If we had taped his behavior on our cell phone, he would have been embarrassed and perhaps attempted to conceal his public behavior in a comparable situation. We must learn to control our public anger, frustration, and demeanor, as they can come back to haunt us later. We could say that he forgot who he was, whether he was a believer, or where he was. Customers were caught in an angry grip with an individual who had become so frustrated that he was no longer in control of his emotions, behaving loudly, upsettingly, and demandingly, while also threateningly. Still, the person he spoke to maintained their composure and gave him alternatives to correct the problem. Finally, he calmed down and began collaborating with her. As we stood in line waiting for our turn, I began to think: what if she treated him the way he treated her—barraging a colleague, threatening to take his business elsewhere, loud, boastful, and unkind? The person was extraordinarily kind and patient under duress. I think each person present was glad that the individual provided service in a businesslike and professional manner. This was perhaps an excellent lesson for those observing role modeling during a time of great self-restraint. Would either of you have carried yourselves with such professionalism? This could have been one of Satan's storms, but God interceded and demonstrated what a believer must do. The individual did not allow Satan to influence them; they emanated a Christlike life stance. You must learn to conceal your public image, fueled by anger and frustration, so that it does not come back to haunt you later. You are living examples for others to see. I recall former Vice President Kamala Harris was called some very hostile and harsh words, referring to her ethnicity, education, position, and culture, simply out of fear. This behavior toward her was not Christlike, but she acted professionally and as a good role model for thousands of young children, girls, and women. She was confident and maintained her inner strength under the heavy load of racial adversity.

Accessorization

Her tenacity is to be applauded, and the exemplary results enabled her to unite diverse groups of people around a common cause. Her not winning the nomination was not due to her inability but rather to her ethnicity, gender, and unacceptability because of who she is and whom she represents. This will, irrespective of some opinions, be etched into the annals of history for generations to come. I wonder what people's reflections will be.

While there is a grave movement to erase people of color from the books, walls, and annals of history, it will be written that surviving generations not yet born or unheard of will hear of this momentous situation. What a remarkable woman. The impression she left on children and adults will never be erased. There was fear because the woman could not be broken; she remained steadfast. She stood firm in her beliefs, those of the people she represented, and most definitely in the rule of law. What can't be conquered is deemed to be feared. She was called names to distract her, but she held firm, and with the power of prayer of the righteous, she persevered until the end. We don't know what happened and probably never will. But an all-seeing and just God can see through walls, and in due time, an all-wise God with a divine presence and unlimited power will ensure that truth prevails.

Scenario 2

Getting our accessories together for inner and outer wear does not always come easily, and sometimes makes prioritizing difficult. While others point out flaws in our character, we remain unaware of how words can affect, sometimes even destroy, another human being. After the workshop, I shared with participants an experience I had at a local restaurant on the way to the venue. Several women shared a meal and discussed their experiences caring for persons with special needs. The first names of the individual and the care provider were shared during their conversation. It sounds like a discussion aimed at gathering information to better understand the process of managing the individual without sharing any private details. One of the women spoke with compassion and concern for

Accessorizing Your Christian Character and Self-Absorbed Nature

the person. I finished my meal and exited the restaurant, heading for my hotel to prepare for my meeting. I began my session the following day by sharing my experience. I stated that as a provider, one should never discuss an individual or others in an open setting, as it is impossible to know who is watching and listening. Those settings can become significantly problematic when people's names are dropped in what is assumed to be a harmless context, such as a ladies' room, a restaurant, a beauty salon, or a local store. I took a restroom break; I headed straight to the facilities, hoping for some personal time. While in the stall, I deeply contemplated whether to let the ladies know I was there when a few others came in. A conversation ensued; it seemed very interesting. I raised my feet to avoid being noticed. One woman suggested they check the stall to see if anyone else was in the bathroom. I was the subject of the conversation. I was so tickled that I could barely contain myself. One remarked about the number of policies and guidelines that needed to be shared with them, "who she thought she was, and who had time to read them all anyway. I need to take care of my individuals. All they can do for me is give me my money and leave me alone. I know what I'm doing," the conversation continued. I flushed the toilet and emerged from the stall. They were shocked to see me.

"How long have you been there?"

"Long enough," I remarked. "I just discussed the topic of talking about people in private or public places, and here you all are doing exactly what we said should not be done. You must be mindful of what you say, where you say it, and how it will affect others."

How can we help people change behaviors that are not beneficial to our environment? How can we help them understand the impact of words on another person and what words may reveal about that individual's life? Paul tells you that man's flesh drives the sensual, and God expects you to mature. In the book of 2 Corinthians 13:11, Paul closes his final greetings by stating, "Be joyful." He tells you to grow to maturity, and when you do, you will see and understand the impact of your words. However, you can only grow when you learn to encourage one another and live in harmony and peace. You can ask God for wisdom, knowledge, and understanding. And pray for spiritual discernment. Then, the God of love and peace will be with you.

2. Guard Your Spiritual Barometer

Let your conversation be always full of grace, seasoned with salt, so you may know how to answer anyone.
Col 4:6

Do not let any unwholesome talk come out of your mouths, but only what is helpful for building others up according to their needs, that it may benefit those who listen.
Eph 4:29

These behaviors act as your spiritual barometer, much like a fever raging within your body, alerting you that something is wrong because other parts of your body are affected. Have you recently assessed your actual spiritual temperature? How high was the reading? Did it affect another person negatively, to the point where you had to say, "I'm sorry?" Can you say sorry when you project negative words or display negative feelings toward another human being that may impact others in the same space? Did you recognize the real you? Do you think your barometer reflects the true love and devotion of God? Have you ascertained why you are so angry and why you scapegoat others, particularly those who are different than you? Is there a fear of losing your social and economic status? Is it that you don't want to share the top with anyone else? These feelings, reflected in table 1 below, are not of God and don't reflect Christlikeness.

Table 1	
True Temperature	
Anger	Rage
Vengeance	Frustration
Hostility	Fury

Accessorizing Your Christian Character and Self-Absorbed Nature

What is your actual spiritual temperature? How much frustration and anger does it take to drive you to a state of hostility or anger, which may lead to vengeance or violence? What emotions do you believe are warning signs that an individual may be a danger to others when driving or a danger to themselves? You can't assume he is not a believer, but you can visualize that he is furious and on the road to self-destruction. What spiritual accessories are warranted to help this individual display the qualities God has given each believer in the fruit of the Spirit? These nine characteristics, given to believers by God, are designed to help the body of Christ develop spiritual disciplines and enhance the believer's Christian lifestyle, ultimately leading to spiritual maturity.

Your temperament must be more like Christ's. Think of all the suffering Christ endured on his way to the cross. Remember the pain of being whipped all night long? Of being accused of things he had not done? He was innocent of all charges; he was mistreated, yet he did not say a mumbling word. But on the cross, after being pierced in his side, spikes driven in his feet, nails driven in his hands, given vinegar to soothe his tongue and quench his thirst—what did he say? Did he show anger? No. Did he portray fear or frustration? No. Did he curse them? This was not his character; what did he say? "Father, forgive them, for they know not what they do." Could any of you have done this? He even took the time to offer salvation to a dying thief. What love! God expects you to learn to walk together and to be kind to your fellow drivers; the life you save may be your own. You may need to accept what is wrong for right. My dad had a saying: "Sister, you can be dead right." The Bible instructs us in Ps 37:8 to refrain from anger, turn from wrath, and not fret, because these actions lead only to evil. You have seen and heard the outcome of road rage fueled by anger and frustration. Perhaps just being overwhelmed by life's circumstances.

According to the *American Heritage Dictionary*, anger is "a strong feeling of displeasure or hostility. . . . The nouns [anger, rage, fury, ire, wrath, resentment, and indignation] denote varying degrees of marked displeasure. *Anger*, the most general, is strong

Accessorization

and often heated displeasure: *[she] shook her fist in anger; [she] retorted in anger at the insult; [she] tried to suppress his anger over the treatment he had received.*"[3] The ingredient mix adds savor to the believer's feelings, and unlike salt, the savor does not automatically dissipate. It takes prayer, a close walk, a deep relationship, and fellowship with God. Paul mentions some of these same ingredient mixes in Gal 5:15–17 (KJV): "But if you bite and devour one another, take heed that ye be not consumed one of another. This I say then, walk in the Spirit, and ye shall not fulfill the lust of the flesh." This advice from Paul may seem simplistic, but it requires effort to put into practice. In today's culture, this Scripture may shape your faith because the written word often differs from the practice. You must constantly be reminded and prayerfully guided by your faith culture that the things that come out of your being, such as your attitude, words, expressions, and thoughts, whether good or bad, positive or negative, reveal what is hidden in the broken chambers of your heart. You must never forget those words, speech, thoughts, and attitudes that serve as your spiritual barometer.

As believers, you too can become entangled in the snares of evil; therefore, you must be mindful of your thoughts, which can lead to wrongdoing. I am reminded of a work situation where the person in charge was complicated and self-righteous, appearing to thirst for setting barriers to others' goals. This individual did not have much respect for women in general, particularly for those who were intelligent, educated, and self-assured, as they seemed to challenge his ego. I recalled his demeanor, and it was so very repellent. My inner thoughts were to rush him, push him and his chair out of the window. Each time I requested to leave the situation, feeling my inner self becoming more agitated, he would say, "I am not done." My response was, "I need to leave this room." Finally, another person sharing the space told him, "She needs to leave." This individual was probably the first "self-righteous narcissist" I met during the earlier years of my career.

You are confronted in this century with an array of self-righteous individuals working in positions that harm the greater

---

3. *The American Heritage Dictionary*, "Anger."

society while benefiting the needs and interests of a few who follow orders out of fear of self-righteous narcissism. You must pray and ask God to help you deal with those individuals who thrive on attention, whether positive or negative, and bring the situation under control so you can move on to the next chapter. You must remember that "silence is golden." If you can train yourself to ignore these personalities, it may not be very easy, but you will be much further ahead. It is a challenging task, and your human nature gets the best of you while these folks keep rolling along. These individuals have broken their oneness with God and their relationship with him by disobeying his instructions.

You are often tempted to respond to the perpetrator similarly, and in my younger, spiritually immature days, I did. As I matured in the word of God and grew in knowledge and understanding, I am now able, with the aid of the Holy Spirit, to pause, reflect, and breathe before acting. In Prov 7:1–5, you are given profound instructions to follow, guard, and obey commands for your life. You must guard those instructions just as you guard your eyes and know how to care for them. He further instructs you to write them deep in your heart. This lets you see the value and importance of what God tells you. If these are written deep in your heart, you will remember them; like your eyes, they are equally valuable to your livelihood.

These elements reveal your accurate temperature regarding your love and devotion to God. It is often said and repeated that what is in a person will come out of them at the most inopportune time. Let you keep your hand in God's hand, so that if those circumstances arise, and they will, God, through the Holy Spirit, will guide, lead, and hold you close, so that self will not allow you to be consumed. In the book *Experiencing God: Knowing and Doing the Will of God*, authors Henry Blackaby, Richard Blackaby, and Claude King tell you that whenever you depart from God in any degree, "he disciplines you in increasing measure until you return to him. God loves you as his child and, as your heavenly Father, will correct you until it reaches a point of crisis at which you must make a serious choice. You cry out to God in your time of distress."[4] As you

---

4. Blackaby et al., *Experiencing God*, 251.

look at all the calamities in the world, immoral behaviors, hypocrisy, idolatry, lack of integrity, greed, grief, and discomfort of man's inhumanity to man, slanderous gossip that separates families, friends, and countries, the world is crying out to God for comfort amid what are becoming darker times. Some are wondering, "Has God forsaken us? Why are these things happening? How can someone take over a country, circumvent the rule of law, and the highest court in the land?" The list is endless. "How?" you asked. God sees, knows, and understands everything. He has not forgotten or forsaken you; he is gracious, merciful, trustworthy, reasonable, and mighty; he has all power, and is still in control. He is waiting for you, his people, the believers, to call on him repeatedly to believe in his power. You must obey his will and his way; like the Israelites, you strayed, perpetuating persistent disobedience. Your heart has become hardened to the word and voice of God, and you continue to do your own thing, your way, and are disobedient. Still, your loving Father is letting you know that the book of Revelation is being fulfilled. You wonder why so many people appear to get away with so much. You must fear your God; he will protect you, strengthen you, and forgive your many sins because he loves you. You must continue to serve him, seek forgiveness for your thoughts, and learn to forgive others. God is the only one who can take revenge. You must be responsible for your thoughts and actions to truly believe God's word. God clearly tells us in this litany of instructions that "then if my people who are called by my name will humble themselves and pray and seek my face and turn from their wicked ways, I will hear from heaven and will forgive their sins and restore their land" (2 Chr 7:14 NLT). He requires humility, prayer, seeking his face, and repentance from your wicked and un-Christlike ways. God will hear your cry, forgive your sins, and bring restoration.

Like David, there are ways an individual can guard their mind and heart and stay spiritually healthy—when all else fails, take flight. This is what David did when Saul pursued him. Run until the Lord directs you to a haven and then gives you further instructions when the pathway is safe. Consider linking up with people who believe in God's word, read and study it, and are positive role

Accessorizing Your Christian Character and Self-Absorbed Nature

models. Reading, meditating, and studying the word of God have answers that go beyond your wildest dreams. The word of God has answers to any situation on earth; all you need to do is search, study, and read, and the answer is there. It may not be the one you want to hear, but God responded.

Paul tells you that the fervent prayer of the righteous has availed much. You must continue to pray in and out of season. Paul also shares with you in Phil 3:15 (NLT) that when you become spiritually mature, you can agree on some things. If you disagree with specific points, God will make the points clear to you. In Phil 3:18–19 (NLT), Paul says, "For I have told you often before, and I say it again with tears in my eyes, that there are many whose conduct shows they are really enemies of the Cross of Christ." Paul continues, "That these individuals are headed for destruction in that their god is their appetite, they brag about shameful things, and they think only about their life on earth." This accessorization, perceived power and control, wealth, brute force, lying, and destroying are all for naught; they will not get anyone into God's kingdom. As you read and hear these verses from Paul's writing, you are reminded of the many challenges facing the country and the many challenges in your own life. You can look back at the Old and New Testaments and see many examples. It seems shameful and causes you to question what appears to be a lack of humanity, a lack of respect for God's law, and disobedience to the rules and commands in the Bible provided for humanity. The Lord tells us in Ezek 7:8–9 (NIV), "I am about to pour out my wrath on you and spend my anger against you; I will judge you according to your conduct and repay you for all your detestable practices. I will not look upon you with pity or spare you . . . then you will know it is I, the Lord, who strikes the blow." God's words are apparent and concise. God does not make empty promises. The consequence for disobedience is when God pours out his wrath upon humanity. This is divine judgment, when he will spend or disburse his anger on you according to your conduct. You, as a believer, should have some sense of what your conduct has been like regarding keeping with his commands and other expectations. God will repay you for all your detestable, abominable, hateful, vile, immoral, and despicable practices—these are all life-altering circumstances because of humanity's abominations and continuous disobedience. This passage of Scripture reveals the consequences of God's anger and retribution. Paul states that, "You are citizens of heaven, and eventually, God will bring everything under his authority and control" (1 Cor 15:27–28).

a. Anger

Everyone should be quick to listen, slow to speak, and slow to become angry because anger does not produce the righteousness that God desires.

JAS 1:19–20 NLT

Prov 15:18 (NIV) states a *hot-tempered man stirs up dissension, but a patient man calms a quarrel.*

In the book of Colossians, anger is described as a feeling of extreme displeasure, hostility, or exasperation toward someone or something (Col 3:8). Other words associated with anger include "wrath," "enrage," "provoke," and "fury." Anger is a strong emotion of irritation or agitation that occurs when a need or expectation is not met.[5] As cited in W. E. Vine, in the Old Testament, anger is most frequently depicted in the Hebrew word "*aph*," literally meaning "nose or nostrils," figuratively depicting nostrils flaring with anger.[6] The above Scriptures eloquently describe the individual scenario in the following event.

Scenario 3

Standing in line at a local store for an excessive amount of time is like having a tea kettle on a burner without a monitor. After an extended

---

5. Hunt, *Anger*, 43.
6. Vine et al., *Vine's Complete Expository*, s.v. "Nose."

Accessorizing Your Christian Character and Self-Absorbed Nature

period, frustration breeds anger, anger fuels hostility, hostility courts rage, and rage attempts to hold vengeance and fury in check. Many of us completed our shopping in this scenario and waited in line to pay for the items. While three people were assigned to assist with checkout, one customer needed help with several items. This issue eventually pulled the other two clerks into the situation. It went on and on and on. I cannot attest to how long the six people in front of me had been waiting, but the behavior and attitude of one of the individuals suggested it must have been a long time. The line had not moved, and it kept getting longer. Finally, a customer in front of me yelled at the cashier, asking what was taking so long and how many people it took to solve the problem. "I have been standing here for more than forty-five minutes," he continued. No one else waiting in line was complaining. We all, however, had choices: either wait or leave. The cashier did not respond, so he approached the cashier and inquired. The customer, who experienced a problem at checkout, said gently and calmly, "You must have patience." The individual blew up, telling her he was not talking to her. He was talking to the cashier, who apologized as well. This did not make him feel any better. He was standing in front of me, walking back to his cart, and mumbling to himself. My stomach tightened as I heard, observed, and experienced his anger. I immediately thought about how this disruptive behavior had led to shouting and how it could have escalated further. A simple issue had now become an uncontrollable rage. It was evident that the customer's anger may have been suppressed or unresolved, and this particular situation was the volcanic fuel that set him off and led him to target this woman. Once his anger let loose, it was on a fast roll straight downhill, poised to hit anything in its way.

Think of anger as high-octane fuel. Pour it directly on a fire, and you'll create an explosion that damages everything nearby.[7] And because of this hurt or a feeling of injustice, his anger erupted like a volcano. The woman was speaking to her friend, who was shopping with her and was noticeably becoming uncomfortable. The woman, however, maintained her composure. The man

---

7. Sun, *Master Anger Management for Success*.

Accessorization

appeared annoyed that the woman had not let his behavior upset her, so he rushed back to the register and exhibited the same annoying behavior. She said again, "Patience, patience, my friend." He began screaming and yelling and calling her an unpleasant name. She maintained her composure. We looked at each other in disbelief and quietly wondered where this behavior was going. It had now escalated to name-calling. He had worked himself into a frenzy and wondered how to vindicate himself by trying to scapegoat her. We all appeared to be holding our breath. There were more women than men from different ethnic groups waiting in line, looking at each other, and probably praying or wishing the line would move. What was he going to do next? The store opened another register to my left, and a male rushed over. The man returned to his original position in line and said, "You can get in front of me. Go ahead." I said, "Oh no, I'm fine. I don't mind waiting." The woman to my left said, "You could go to the line over there," and I said, "No, you go ahead. I am fine." I did not want the man behind me or beside me. I felt safer with him before me, and it was just fine. He finally reached the register; there was no conversation between him and the cashier beyond what was necessary. Most of us were very proud of the young woman who did not allow herself to be pulled into the man's circle of anger and frustration, thereby rewarding his ego. He made himself look foolish, and no one in line succumbed to his raging displays of anger, hostility, and frustration. While leaving the store, I observed the young woman near her car and commended her for her demeanor, strength, and attitude. Because of his anger, she could have been involved in a severe altercation; however, she demonstrated great constraint under pressure. She continued to repeat, "We must have patience; we must have patience." The woman was a believer and did not allow her flesh to overshadow her spiritual character. She could have become angry when the man called her anything other than her name, but she held firm.

  Anger has many accessories, and if you are not careful, you can quickly be drawn into its accessorized behaviors, including hostility, yelling, screaming, profanity, and probably rage. She

Accessorizing Your Christian Character and Self-Absorbed Nature

could have been easily provoked into participating in public conflict if she were not spiritually mature. These ingredients, when mixed, contribute to the scene described above and could have been quickly illustrated by the language of the male contributor alone. His language, provoked by anger and frustration, was unacceptable. If we listened carefully to the man's words and observed his body language, we might wonder what happened yesterday or last night that spilled over into today. If this woman had not been a child of God, she could have been tomorrow's headline. There is joy in knowing the Lord and peace in forgiveness. God can use a pure heart and a clean spirit. You cannot allow anger to destroy your opportunity for everlasting life with God. A moment of anger can lead to a lifetime of bitter and life-altering consequences. Does your anger and insecurity lead you to make negative statements about another person? In an angry rage, someone directed negative statements at and about you. As you review each negative statement below, consider how you would feel if those statements were made about or directed at you. Negative messages that may hinder your spiritual growth and impact your spiritual walk must be avoided and alleviated. In the same context, has there ever been a time when you may have needed to suppress the truth to prevent others from knowing and seeing the real you?

Table 2. Negative vs. Positive Statements	
Negative Statement	**Positive Statement**
You drive me up a brick wall.	I am upset about your attitude. When you've calmed down, we'll talk.
If your mother heard what you did, girl, she would be disappointed.	Your mother does not appreciate or approve of your behavior.
You make me sad. You are such a disappointment.	I am angry with you right now.
Don't feel so angry; you look stupid.	It's OK to feel that way, but I want you to manage your feelings. Let's talk.
You hurt my feelings! I am so disappointed in you.	I feel hurt.

Accessorization

Table 2. Negative vs. Positive Statements	
Negative Statement	**Positive Statement**
Now you have done it. Take your ugly butt and sit in that corner. See if you can learn some sense.	She is crying. Please leave her alone for a few minutes.
Try to make me proud of you, son.	I am so proud of you, my son. You did an excellent job.
Don't let your old man down, son.	Please do this for yourself, not for me. I will always love you and be proud of you.
You make me feel like such a failure as your mother.	I feel so sad about your friend. If you'd like to talk, I'm available.
You are so stupid, like your dumb-butt father.	Some of your behaviors are difficult to deal with; we need to find other alternatives for you to express your feelings.
That's why nobody loves you.	You are a wonderful child, but sometimes it's challenging to deal with your anger.
Get your dumb butt out of my sight. I wouldn't say I like looking at you right now.	We need a little space between us until I can compose myself.
You aren't worth beans.	You are my child, and I love you.
You are just ruining the image of the Black family with another child born out of wedlock.	Life continues when you choose to have a baby and are unmarried; you can continue your education, graduate, or, if you decide to attend college, earn your degree and pursue your dreams.

Developed by Doris A. Bourgeois Turner, 2023

    You must understand the nature of your anger and what kindles it within you so that you can transform it into a glowing, uncontrollable flame, like a raging fire. Hunt tells you in her book that you must analyze your anger to understand where, what, and why the anger began, as well as what precipitated the rage within, why it got out of control, but also how to prevent it and how to control it should it break out again.[8] What accessories are required

---

8. Hunt, *Anger*, 51.

to get this rage under control, and how do you contain those emotions so they do not erupt again? Through the aid of the Holy Spirit that dwells within your temple and is with you 24/7, your inner anger, rage, frustrations, and other emotions are contained and held in check, and you must play your part.

If the man in the store had reflected on his behavior, he might have realized that the woman was just an obstacle to his explosive fuse. She deflected the delayed experience that left him very frustrated, similar to a post-traumatic stress disorder (PTSD) flashback. How can he reverse those emotions with love, patience, kindness, and understanding, aligning God's purpose and expectations for his life? Suppose you don't find appropriate sources to express your feelings and allow yourself to continue on this path. In that case, your outbursts may eventually cause you to self-destruct, resulting in losing relationships and perhaps even your fellowship with God. The Bible tells you in Matt 5:22 that anyone who is angry with his brother will be subject to judgment. That is why you are encouraged not to let the sun set without seeking peace with each other.

Many of you have read the biblical story about Cain and Abel in Gen 4:2. Abel was a shepherd, and Cain cultivated the ground. When it was time for the harvest, Cain gave some of his crops as a gift to God, while Abel brought the best portion of the firstborn lambs from his flock. God accepted Abel's gift but not Cain's. Cain was furious and dejected. God asked him why and told Cain that he would be accepted when he did what was right, but rejected when he did not watch out. "Sin is crouching at his door and is eager to control him. But it is up to Cain to subdue the sin and be its master." Here it is both an accessory of envy and of jealousy. These will indeed cause you to fall if you do not pray and ask the Holy Spirit to help you rid yourselves of this animosity, which can develop into deep-seated feelings of dislike, hatred, or even resentment. God did tell him that sin was "crouching at his door," and he needed to control it. Cain, however, allowed his jealousy to build into angry feelings, overshadowing his ability to accept and do what was right. He encouraged his brother to come to the fields, and while there, he killed his brother. Cain then lied to God, claiming he did not know where Abel was, and asked, "Am I my brother's keeper?" God persisted and said to Cain, "What have you done?" God told Cain that Abel's blood was crying out to him (God). God cursed Cain and banished him from the ground and the presence of God. Can you imagine having God himself tell you that you are banished from his presence? This meant he was forever expelled and could not return. Other people in the Bible received punishment, beginning with Adam and Eve, because of their disobedience; Cain was doomed to wander because he did not control his anger and subsequently allowed his emotions to cause him to take the life of his brother. Other instances in the Bible: Kings were banished by God, people of Judah were exiled from their land by God, Saul expelled mediums and spirits from the land, and Asa banished shrine prostitutes from the land. Banishment is a harsh punishment, and in all the situations cited above, people like Cain brought it upon themselves by failing to listen and obey. God warned Cain to control himself, or sin would take over. Are you, in some respect, like Cain, allowed to correct a flaw in your character that may reunite your *koinonia* with God? Anger led Cain to commit foolish and evil acts, resulting in life-altering changes for him and his brother. In Jas 1:19, you are told that you must be quick to listen, slow to speak, and slow to get angry. Human anger does not produce the righteousness God desires. You must learn to listen, believe, trust, and have faith to follow as you accept with humility the word God has planted in your heart, for it has saving grace and power to keep you from falling into a dark place, and if not rooted in his word, can continue to fall into the abyss.

b. Rage

Fools vent their rage, but the wise bring calm in the end.
PROV 29:11

Accessorizing Your Christian Character and Self-Absorbed Nature

Understand this, my dear brothers and sisters: You must all be quick to listen, slow to speak, and slow to anger. Human anger does not produce the righteousness God desires.

Jas 1:19–20

According to the *Collins English Dictionary,* rage is intense anger that is difficult to control.[9] It is uncontrolled explosive emotions accompanied by violent anger with furious intensity. It is more justifiable by circumstances. Paul discusses rage as another temperament, personality, character, or disposition in which this emotion becomes intense. Like with the above ingredient, filthy language was directed at another person, just as the man did in the local store when he allowed his anger to elevate to rage. The sin of rage is "wrath (*ira*), which can be defined as uncontrolled feelings of anger, rage, and even hatred. Wrath often reveals itself in the wish to seek vengeance."[10] How many ingredients can you identify that are reflected in this store scenario? Ask yourself, at what range did the temperature reach a state of emotional rage? Remember how the man's feelings seemed out of character? He resorted to calling the lady a derogatory name, but she did not allow herself to buy into his angry, raging state. Perhaps this was part of God's plan. Had she heard him, I don't know what the repercussions might have been. Her demeanor and character were respectful and dignified. This woman demonstrated inner peace by simply saying, "You've got to have patience." Was she reassuring herself about patience, or letting him know that patience would bring him calmness and peace, and save his public self? She was the better person in the situation. The woman did not let the man's explosive and embarrassing circumstances rob her of her dignity and self-respect. Remember, you don't know who is watching your public behavior.

    Over the past few years, many of you have witnessed the deterioration of societal values, morals, Christian virtues, and respect for those outside the elite class, where wealth, influence, and

9. *Collins Dictionary,* "Rage."
10. Wikipedia, "Seven Deadly Sins."

Accessorization

power rule. As you continued to listen to the rhetoric, you heard how people's names were smeared; people's lives were threatened when some members of a political party believed that second-class citizens, particularly people of color and those of a particular socioeconomic status, threatened their form of social standards. You consistently hear of retribution against those members of society who believe differently. Sometimes, you may have wondered, "Where is God, and why is he allowing this to happen?" Indeed, he sees what is happening in his world. You know he is still in control, and you hear his voice reminding you that he is still with you. If you recall in Scripture, the wheat and tares will grow together and will be separated in due time.

When President Biden withdrew from the 2024 Democratic primary, it was assumed that another Democrat would run, so the plan could have been to refocus and run against that candidate. However, this did not appear to be the case. The opponent was now running against a younger, intelligent, educated, sophisticated, respected, independent, and highly qualified Black Asian American woman. She was personable, experienced in debating politics, and knew and believed in the rule of law. With God's divine will, Vice President Kamala Harris forged forward, fulfilling a prophecy that the late Shirley Chisholm hoped to accomplish or that Hillary Rodham Clinton believed she could have secured. Because of her abilities, tenacity, and knowledge, VP Harris appeared to be a threat and became the object of name-calling, mean-spirited racial slurs, and bigotry. Some members of society seem to have never learned checks and balances or boundaries. Some individuals have used the Fourteenth Amendment to justify and attempt to legalize their right to express themselves as they want, and to whom they wish, without fear of repercussions. This was perpetuated in the legal system until it went too far, necessitating the use of the "rule of law" to establish some guidelines and boundaries. While the Fourteenth Amendment protects the right of free speech, it also guards against its abuse when it is directed and used as a deliberate weapon.

When historians not yet born look back over this century, they will wonder how someone who faced profound legal implications

Accessorizing Your Christian Character and Self-Absorbed Nature

in the states of Washington, Georgia, New York, and Florida delayed paying for these legalities or was tried by the legal system, and was yet able to run for president of the United States and win. It is baffling to observe how many citizens still believe in the concept of the individual. Would the same scenario have applied if the individual had been a man of color or an ordinary citizen? You determine. The legal system suggests that, in some instances, it aligns more with the interests of the wealthy and powerful than with people of color or the rule of law, and not even for the sake of righteousness. Only God will bring a fair and just ending to this scenario. Man is incapable, and the stakes appeared too high for those who know the truth and what was right and just. Propaganda seemed to prevail; the belief system was marred by untruths, half-truths, and falsehoods that had been made to seem true, and the beast that lies within continued to grow and become stronger with the accompaniment of deceit, fear of retribution and retaliation, loss of power, and greed. If deductive reasoning does not prevail, and it appears it will not, God will make the final judgment call; he sits in judgment daily and knows the accurate or actual plumb line. He tells you in his written words that vengeance is his, yet some individuals continue to seek retribution. The words are harsh, chilling, and vengeful. What is next, one wonders. The book is not completed, and the election is over. It did not go as millions of voters had anticipated, and there appears to be uncertainty about the "Make America Great Again" (MAGA) movement's Electoral College victory. There is a deep-rooted feeling that unfairness may be possible, but this has not yet been proven. The results are in God's hands. Believers know that God is in control. Life has become a bit uncertain, with danger looming ahead. Families are finding that prices are constantly increasing, and jobs are being eliminated at the every level in both the private and public sectors. Family life may become dysfunctional, especially given the lack of notice, preventing people from adjusting to a different lifestyle. People who took a stand on the letter of the law or stood against criminality, injustices, unrighteousness, suspected fraud, and other accessories discussed by Paul in Scripture are now caught up in a "catapult" of retributive circumstances. Those of you who are believers in the word of God may wonder how these people, who are fathers and mothers, lawyers and doctors, senators and congressmen, sat indolently by as though they were caught up in an invisible web, secretly wishing things would go away or return to a web of normalcy. Can you honestly say they are believers and are praying? This thought may be judgmental, yet one wonders because it lends itself to accessories like consciousness, a thought process that forces one to open their eyes to truth, feelings, and emotions. A sense of compassion is not what appears to be transmitted; fear, anger, and hate are the visible elements that are evident. With such signs, you must continue to let go and let God; let him have his way; he will wipe away the painful tears and disappointment of the innocent. Unrighteousness and transgressions will not prevail.

c. Vengeance

I will execute terrible vengeance against them to punish them for what they have done. And when I have afflicted my revenge, they will know that I am the Lord.
EZEK 25:17–18 NLT

We are told in Lev 19:18–19 (NLT): "Do not seek revenge or bear a grudge against a fellow Israelite, but love your neighbors as yourself. I am the Lord. You must obey all my decrees."

Who are you to decide that you will have vengeance on another human being because they do not think or act as you do? You have allowed yourself to become vengeful because you cannot persuade people to do wrong. You reject citizens who are economically and socially deprived. You must remember that you cannot control a situation or people unless they surrender their rights and support the cause. The Lord declared that vengeance is his, and at his time and discretion, he will take vengeance, as noted in Scripture, on those who disobey his commands and do injustices that cause the body of Christ to suffer. The Lord tells you in his words that there are things that he hates. As believers in the word of God, remember that the rage that you sometimes feel within only leads you to tragedy, and you fall further and further away from your *koinonia* (fellowship) and oneness with God. The newly elected president sometimes describes people he hates—such a strong word—as being rejected from his fellowship. You cannot have *koinonia* with God and hate your brothers and sisters who are different than you or are not as financially secure as you or as educated or who believe in fairness and humanity. You will be rejected from God's fellowship and his presence, as Cain experienced when he took the life of his brother.

Prov 6:16–19 (KJV): *God provides a list of those behaviors that he cannot tolerate or hate*:

a. "proud look or proud eyes,
b. lying tongue,
c. hand that shed innocent blood,
d. a heart that devised wicked imaginations,
e. a set of feet that be swift in running to mischief,
f. false witness that speaketh lies; and a
g. person who soweth discord among brethren."

As you ponder this list of accessories God hates, and "hate" is such a strong word, do you find yourself hedging on any of these accessories? Have you found yourself amid challenges that make you wonder if you have displeased God in any of these areas? Have you created conditions that cause a brother or sister to stumble due to jealousy, envy, fear, or a lack of knowledge, wisdom, or understanding? Have you stopped to reflect on your schedule of unnecessary activities that may have nothing to do with kingdom-building for God, but instead for yourself? Where were you during the election and its aftermath? Have you prayed and asked God to show you the way, or are you running on emotions and adrenaline, seeing things from your narrow perspective? What was best for the greater good? There were those persons whom Scripture references

Accessorization

as being "morally perverse" or having a "reprobate" mind. Have you stopped to reflect on these characteristics to determine if it is I, Lord? Can you honestly ask the Lord to remove from you any of these characteristics or accessories if he finds them in you? Because it is your goal to live and maintain a Christlike character. Have you wondered if not supporting a woman, and a woman of color, would increase the likelihood of losing the election? Were your thoughts and ability to process information rationally, clearly, and objectively clouded by fear, doubt, anger, or misinformation? As you reflect on and ponder everything that has occurred since the inauguration, does it cause you to wonder what, if anything, did you do? Reflection can be frightful. It can reveal the ugly truths. Where are you now? How vital were self-will, desires, and your self-interests or your personal agenda designed for your benefit?

Mulholland wonderfully states those above factors "regulated your existence. Everything was about you and your needs."[11] Are you perhaps thinking and feeling like Paul—no matter what you do to be righteous, following God's will, wanting to do what is right, evil is always there (Rom 7:23 KJV)? Was Paul struggling with sin in Romans chapter seven and as he cried out to God in verse 24, "O wretched man that I am! who shall deliver me from the body of this death?" Are you like the Sabal palmetto palm, which has a flexible trunk that bends with the wind, preventing it from snapping and allowing it to sway, thereby strengthening its roots over time? Is this what occurred with some believers? After hearing the rhetoric, it became believable and acceptable, thereby taking root in their every being. Or perhaps like the turtle that sits on its comfortable rock in the middle of the pond, until it hears something, unwilling to become involved, it draws its head into its shell and remains there until it assumes the circumstance is over. Others may have characteristics similar to the live oak. You stay resistant to the damage of rhetoric through prayer and supplication because your foundation is strong, built on a solid rock that provides sustenance to hold on and hold out. You are attached to the accessories found in Heb 6:10–12.

---

11. Mulholland, *Invitation to a Journey*, 45.

d. Frustration or Being Dismayed

Those who control their anger have a great understanding; those with a hasty temper will make mistakes.

Prov 14:29

In Ps 37:8, *we are told not to be anxious about anything but to present your requests to God in every situation by prayer and petition, with thanksgiving.*

Dismayed "is experiencing or showing feelings of alarmed concern or dismay: being upset, worried, or agitated because of some unwelcome situation or occurrence."[12] In the Holy Bible, the term "frustration" derives from "'frustrate' (from frustra, 'vain') and is the translation of parar, 'to break,' 'to make void,' 'to bring to nothing' (Ezra 4:5), 'to frustrate their purpose' (Isa 44:25, 'that frustrateth the signs of the liars')."[13]

Before the COVID-19 pandemic, some people appeared short-tempered and intolerant of issues or circumstances. However, post-COVID-19, there seemed to be less tolerance for many things and more frustration over minor issues. Driving on the highway can become a death sentence if you unconsciously cut someone off or look at another driver questioningly, with facial expressions or body language that may indicate, "That was a dumb thing to do," or perhaps, "How stupid, you could have caused an accident." These circumstances are like fuel that ignites a slow-burning candle. These elements can become sins against God due to your behavior and a lack of love and compassion for others. Many of you seem bottled up, holding anger, fear, frustration, insecurities, uneasiness, and misunderstanding in your spirits. Even some pulpits, during their sermons, seem to offer more personal and inner turmoil and less encouragement, comfort, and support to their members than in years past. There is an appearance of

---

12. *Merriam-Webster*, "Dismayed."
13. Walker, "Frustrate."

Accessorization

directing inner frustrations and shortcomings rather than conveying a sense of pastoral care, one that is nurturing and concerned about the wellbeing of the congregation's members. Sometimes there is a sense of preaching at the congregation rather than sharing words that will help members persevere, feel a sense of belonging, and feel welcomed. Imagine how Jesus must have felt when he was barraged by the crowd seeking his very words for healing and deliverance, support and direction, prayer and understanding, repentance and compassion, love and kindness—he admonished transgressions but never the transgressors. He did not alienate his followers as some believers may do; he accepted the sinner and forgave the sin. This is what Jesus did with the woman who was about to be stoned for her sins. He said, "Go and sin no more."

As Paul writes in Gal 6:2, "Bear one another's burdens, and so fulfill the law of Christ." Just as Jesus moved away physically from the crowd, there are times when the minister needs to seek divine support to deal with their mental, emotional, moral, and psychological distress. This will give the minister a different perspective and physical outlet for their stressors. The ability to "move away" creates a safe haven to communicate with God, allowing them to reposition their focus and better prepare themselves to meet the challenge of the position, which is greater now than ever before. Ministers are human beings too, and often suffer from member overload, which can be overwhelming (Eph 4:11–17). God gave pastors, apostles, prophets, evangelists, and teachers to prepare his people for kingdom work so that the body of Christ may be built up. It is the minister's responsibility to maintain spiritual wellbeing, live a life worthy of his calling, and strive to maintain unity in the body of Christ.

Just as you use a wet wipe or an Olay oil sheet to remove makeup and dirt from your face, you must accept the word of God in your heart and repeat a mantra, a Bible verse, or some form of spirituality to guide you through the day. Just as you shower each morning or night to relieve the dread and frustration of the day, to clean and release tension and pain from your physical body, you must do the same for your spiritual body through prayer and

Accessorizing Your Christian Character and Self-Absorbed Nature

supplication to God. These feelings and emotions of frustration and tension are but from the devil, who spends his time aggravating and upsetting God's children. He is not interested in the nonbeliever; he already has them in his grasp. He is after God's children, the believers, those who trust God and have faith in him and his promises. Do you recall Job, minding his own business, a child of God, but this did not negate Satan being after him? You accessorize the material; you must also accessorize the spiritual.

I share with you the story of a baby lizard trapped on the screened back porch. This story illustrates the homeowner's frustration, fear, compassion, and hopelessness. We are not particularly fond of the little lizards, as they are everywhere. We don't wish to harm them, but they are a general nuisance. Since I am not too familiar with them, I avoid them at all costs. This little lizard drew our compassion and concern. It was a beautiful Saturday morning; the sun shone over the backyard, and the screen porch looked inviting. I slowly opened the porch door to ensure no lizards were present. We had not noticed the lizard for a few days and assumed my husband had safely placed him in the backyard. I checked again, and he was indeed on the screened porch. He had not gone out the door as we thought, but had gently slipped back onto the porch. He had now been there for two days. I shared my concern with my husband and assured him that the lizard was still there. The little lizard crawled from screen panel to screen panel, unable to find its way out. It was very hot, and I was unsure how the lizard managed to survive for three days. That morning, a large lizard came to his rescue. As I observed the lizard, he appeared to be trying to coax the baby lizard into a position that would allow it to escape, but the baby lizard was too weak to follow his instructions. After several attempts, the large lizard left, appearing frustrated because the baby lizard would not follow instructions. The baby lizard seemed frantic and abandoned by the other lizard; his emotions and body movements made it appear as if he were crying and calling out for help. In the meantime, another lizard appeared on the screen; it was the same size as him, and he attempted to guide the lizard to the spot where he could escape, but to no avail.

Accessorization

I looked out again, and the baby lizard was back in its comfortable spot, nestled in the coolness of the plant. He sat for a few minutes and then attempted to crawl up to the screen. He appeared to be looking for water but was too weak to crawl. My heart was so sad for the baby lizard. I was too afraid of him to move him myself. The baby lizard must have heard something; it got a surge of energy, and its head moved from side to side as if it were listening, then it moves swiftly. I looked out, and another lizard was on the screen door, calling instructions to the baby lizard, but he ran in the wrong direction. I surmised that he must be disoriented. One of his little friends comes to his rescue and finds himself between the glass and the screen door, but he thinks critically, remains calm, and crawls out. He tried hard to get his friend to do the same thing, but it did not work.

I was now frustrated and concerned about the baby lizard, so my husband gently moved it outside the screened porch onto the patio. In his infinite wisdom, God always sends angels to guide and provide for us when we are at our most vulnerable and weakest. The baby lizard could not follow the other lizards' directions because he was unfamiliar with the path they were directing him to.

Some of you are like the baby lizard or the prodigal son. You stray away from God, going in different directions and experiencing good times, and when all of your resources are gone, people no longer have time for you, and then your circumstances strike you square in the face. You realize you need to head home with your pride beneath you. The baby lizard had friends who tried to help, but he had allowed his circumstances to lead him in the wrong direction and could not move forward on the path home. You must return to God for forgiveness and reestablish your oneness and fellowship with him. The baby lizard needed help escaping his situation, just as you do. Your frustration with life and people can sometimes drive you to seek other alternatives to life's challenges. It becomes very frustrating when you think you have implemented the appropriate standards, guidelines, and expectations, only to be bombarded by unexpected challenges and obstacles in your daily life. You must, however, remember that just because you are a believer and accept Jesus as your Lord and Savior, it does not negate or isolate you from the issues and frustrations in your life. Your success, belief, and commitment to the Lord make you a target for the enemy, who seeks to test you to see if there are any loopholes, such as malice or discord, in your life that can be penetrated. These daily challenges may cause some of you to falter, but you know that you are encouraged to continue to trust in the Lord; your faith is more substantial, deeply rooted, and strongly connected to the Vine, and as branches, you remember through your faith file how God has brought you through time after time. Jesus is the ultimate example of continuous joy for a fulfilled and abundant life. Still, you must be willing to relinquish some things that you cherish to fully understand their meaning. This is not easy. Your life is often filled with unnecessary activities and self-made responsibilities until you think you have arrived. Realizing you are self-absorbed has led you to a hollow wall. You then become angry and frustrated, playing the transference game. Someone else becomes the object to which you release your stored-up emotions in the blame game. Whatever happened that day or the last few minutes is linked to the first person who attracts your attention. I know from experience that even though the individual may have used the phrases "I am sorry" and "Please accept my apology," it does not alleviate the pain I, the victim, have endured. There have been times when I have honestly expressed that I have not accepted their apology. I felt it was not offered in sincerity but as a gesture to make themselves feel better. "I am sorry" has become a cliché. Joshua Choonmin Kang, in his book *Deep-Rooted in Christ: The Way of Transformation*, clarifies that Jesus never promised a comfortable life but an abundant life (John 10:10). An abundant life is a happy life filled with spiritual meaning and worthwhile tasks.[14] As a believer, I know I am not perfect, but I am working through prayer and reading God's word to accept apologies, even when they are not sincere. I am learning to leave these situations in God's hands. It's tough! And there have been some painful moments. It is a daily challenge. I continue to strive. And I cannot

14. Kang, *Deep-Rooted in Christ*, 166.

Accessorization

allow those individuals to ruin my joy, peace, and my relationship with God.

e. Hostility

Paul states in Rom 8:7 (NIV) that the *carnal mind is enmity, and hostile, against God.*

In Eph 2:2 (KJV), he writes *that hostility is motivated by the prince of the power of the air, the spirit that now worketh in the children of disobedience.*

Hostility is "unfriendly or aggressive behavior toward people or ideas."[15] During the 2024 election, there was hostile and aggressive behavior toward candidates of an opposing party, such as name-calling, mispronouncing the opponent's name, and spending money and time trying to secure or solicit negative information about the individual, or attempting to smear the individual's name or destroy their character. This behavior is not acceptable to God. There were reportedly unethical issues that fell outside the rule of law and were unjust in God's eyes. There was also open behavior of hostility, bullying, and threatening people in an unprofessional manner to gain control and power. This was done through attempts to control people's lives by appointing individuals who sought to impede the democratic electoral process. Some reportedly committed willful acts of lawlessness against society and received complete immunity from prosecution. I ask you, what would Jesus do? What does God think about the things you do for personal gain that are not written in his commandments or statutes, in essence, greed? How will he judge those behaviors and actions that have been committed? Scripture instructs you not to add to or subtract from the word of God. The consequences are life-altering. How will God judge those who alter his words and portray themselves in his Bible? I must be honest; there were times I wondered where

---

15. *Collins Dictionary*, "Hostility."

God was. But I realize there are times he allows us to stew in our own mess. Perhaps this is one of those times. I trust and believe in him and know he is right here. I do not doubt his presence or words. Still, frustration, anger, and the un-believability of what I heard on the news, in conversation, or virtually can cloud even the most devout believer's faith. I know that God's timing is not my timing, and he does not need my help. In his own time, he will address the injustices inflicted upon his children through the power of control and fear. I must learn to wait, and as I do, my faith grows stronger. I can't allow myself to be moved by negative emotions from Christlikeness to becoming Christ-unlikeness. This type of behavior can separate me from God.

As Mulholland states, on your spiritual journey, there is a moment of "separation and alienation from God . . . to a transforming relationship with God and wholeness in Christ."[16] This, I believe, is the ultimate goal on your journey from brokenness to wholeness in God. Is God calling you to greater wholeness in him? If you stop for a minute from your busy activities and listen, he may be whispering to you to repent and surrender all those issues, challenges, and circumstances to him. Can you hear the call? What is your response?

f. Fury

Fury is not in me: who would set the briers and thorns against me in battle? I would go through them. I would burn them together. Or let him take hold of my strength, that he may make peace with me; and he shall make peace with me.

Isa 27:4–5 KJV

What is God's fury? God's wrath, in perfect harmony with all his divine attributes, is the holy action of retributive justice towards persons whose actions deserve eternal condemnation. Fury, more destructive than rage, is an outburst of violent anger and rage. The *Collins Dictionary* states, "Fury is unrestrained or violent anger,

16. Mulholland, *Invitation*, 45.

Accessorization

wrath, passion, such as the gods unleashed their fury on the offending mortal."[17] The *International Standard Bible Encyclopedia* states that fu'-ri (Alastor, "not to forget," significant of revenge) occurs in the King James Version, "Thou like fury, (the Revised Version British and American) ("Thou, miscreant") takes you out of this present life."[18] If you have ever been in the midst of a hurricane, sheltering in your home if forecasters have deemed it safe or sitting in a shelter in a school or some other building deemed safe and secure from the storm, you have experienced the fury of the wind bending trees and the raging sound of the rain as it beats against the building, leaving you to wonder if you will see the next day. You can experience the wind and rain beating against the walls of the home or over the roof, making you wonder if it will stand the force of the howling wind. This is similar to some situations you experienced on life's pathway. One could say that there was a fury of anger during the election campaign, with various signs displaying distasteful suggestions or slogans aimed at people of another party or ethnic group. It is sufficient to say that when people feel threatened or believe they are losing control, they may strike back unconventionally. There is a song, "The Lord Will Make A Way Somehow," written by Hezekiah Walker, that is sometimes sung in places of worship or concerts. I would often hear my dad walking around the house, singing this song "fore day in the morning" (means "early in the morning"). He would sing with such fervor, and by his voice, I knew that something was rough, and he was praying through song, asking God to make a way. This song helps me as a believer know and understand that no matter how difficult the road seems, the number of stumbling blocks I must go over or go around or through, the pitfalls dug to deter me, the mere amount of deception other believers and I face each day as followers of Christ. Because of falsehoods, dishonesty, and greed in business and sometimes with people in general, we may find ourselves trapped in their uncanny web, like a spider waiting to trap its unsuspecting prey. Still, we know that through it all, the

17. *Collins Dictionary*, "Fury."
18. *International Standard Bible Encyclopedia Online*, "Fury."

Accessorizing Your Christian Character and Self-Absorbed Nature

Lord will see us through. Our faith file helps us remember that he did it before and can—and will—do it again. God's wrath will prevail (Rom 1:18 KJV). His wrath or fury is not the revelation of a future judgment of God or the great tribulation, but a present revelation that parallels the present revelation of God's righteousness.

Another encouraging song I often think about when things seem overwhelming, and there appears to be no end in sight, is the song written by Charles Albert Tindley in the early 1900s, called "The Storm is Passing Over." Tindley was a Black composer who lived during the turn of the twentieth century and was born in 1851, the son of an enslaved man.

This song appears to provide comfort, console the weary soul, strengthen, and give hope, ultimately increasing the believer's faith during difficult times. Each believer goes through storms and needs to be encouraged when their bodies are overwhelmed by challenges and life circumstances, praying for strength to navigate life's struggles. Rest assured, "God provides anchors for storms."[19] It tells us that God gives us courage to help us along our journey. It helps when it seems like all changes will be life-altering.

3. Conducting Self—Watch That Attitude!

Teach me, and I will be quiet; show me where I have been wrong. How painful are honest words! But what do your arguments prove? Do you mean to correct what I say, and treat the words of a despairing man as wind?

JOB 6:24–26 NIV

---

19. Turner, *God Is a Strong Shelter*, 99.

Accessorization

> I'll get him! I'll show you!
>
> I'll get even with him.
>
> Who does he think he is?
>
> He does not know who I am!
>
> Do you, as a believer, ever scheme to get even?

Do You Harbor Angry, Vengeful Thoughts?

What do these phrases mean to you as a believer in the word of God? How do you remove angry thoughts and feelings from your heart and mind? How do these feelings impact your emotional, psychological, social, and physical wellbeing? Based on Scripture, what does God expect of you in these daily situations? As you read these phrases, consider your behavior, thoughts, and actions toward people who you feel mistreated you or made a negative comment about a relative or a close friend. What is the nature of your anger, frustration, arrogance, hostile inner thoughts, and feelings of getting even? How do these negative thoughts, actions, and emotions impact your fellowship (*koinonia*) with God? How should you act or react under these circumstances?

As you accessorize your spiritual self, look at your feet and where they carry you. Where are you stepping as your toes point forward? What do you think as you lie down where you should not be? Are your toes tingling, trying to tell you to move forward with haste? Have you given it much thought? Is it because you think someone wants to take what you perceive as yours? Does insecurity initiate your fear and frustration? Have you allowed the

Accessorizing Your Christian Character and Self-Absorbed Nature

accessories of jealousy, accompanied by pride and prejudice, to raise their ugly heads and thoughtlessness in your heart? Is it your ego? Or perhaps you fear that your perceived kingdom and power, driven by greed, will tumble because you miscalculated and misunderstood the skills and abilities of another? Some people have lived in bondage and experienced discrimination for a significant portion of their lives, and have no intention of going back. There is a tremendous inner drive to continue moving forward, exploring and enjoying all the benefits life offers in a land of plenty. The struggle has been too hard and long, the sacrifices too extensive, and the pain unthinkable. What is your perception?

If you don't conquer or attempt to understand fear and angry feelings, these tensions and emotions will lead you to self-absorption and self-destruction. You must be courageous and forthright, like Esther. Once she understood her purpose and role in life, prosperity and fame became secondary. Those were self-righteous expectations, and her desire to be greater than she could be. However, through her mentor, Mordecai, she realized she was expected to make a much greater sacrifice for her people. Hers was to meet with the king to save her people from being killed; meeting with the king was not allowed, and she might be killed. Esther said, "If I perish, I perish, but I am going to see the king" (Esth 4:15–16). This teaches you that courage, persistence, prayer, faith, trust, fasting, and obedience to God's divine instructions have spiritual benefits and positive results. Has God called you to serve or given you a specific assignment to build up and edify the body of Christ? Have you responded in obedience to the call, or have you disobeyed God's assigned task because of fear, opinions, or self-will? Disobedience to God's call has serious and life-altering consequences. God is faithful. Are you? God keeps his promises. Do you? What impact did your broken promise(s) have on another believer?

In the Fourth Psalm, the psalmist cries out for God to hear his cry, which is embedded in his inner being. He begs God for deliverance from troubles and the spoils of his reputation based on groundless and unsubstantiated accusations and lies. The psalmist

Accessorization

seeks God's favor to help him so his anger does not control and consume his soul. Have there been times when you found yourself in similar situations? The lies told are unfounded and are so propagandized that you may begin to believe the story yourself. Some of you may be skilled in perfecting your opinions into seemingly proverbial statements that listeners may start to accept. The depth and believability of the statements may depend on your identification and standing within the community. You may try to suppress your emotions, but they inevitably surface. These emotional distresses and psychological issues may persist until an inner life change comparable to your outer lifestyle is developed through prayer, meditation, and supplication to God, seeking and asking him to cleanse your heart, which has been poisoned and shattered by hate and an inferior temperament or complex. The hate is prevalent because you have allowed yourself to be unknowingly scapegoated to pour out your feelings and bestow pain and anger on others. How will this pain impact your family's psychological and social self-esteem and self-confidence? For example, a mom who is dysfunctional because she lived in an environment with her dysfunctional mom. She did not find nor perhaps desire a legitimate way to deal with her pain, and as a result, she consumed her inner self with alcohol and drugs, allowing her outer self to lose control over her environment. Or perhaps lost herself in solicited sexual behavior as a means of escaping her pain, guilt, and grief attributed to loss suffered on her life's journey; if but temporarily, it is a pleasurable way for her to lose herself within momentary feel-good acts. Another mom may begin calling her children names and may become abusive when the emotional pain of her man's absence hurts so deeply. Her grief and loss of self and him, through negative attention, are too overwhelming. She fears striking out at him, so her children or herself becomes the target of her intense emotions. Thus, the child, if a male, may hate women because of their mom's lifestyle, or the daughter may see this behavior as a method of dealing with love and acceptance in future relationships.

A mom may lose focus because her path has become clouded by failure, disappointments, and a lack of success. She is so profoundly impacted by what life has dealt her that she feels God, the Father, Author, and Finisher of her faith—who is her Comforter and sees and knows her trials—has forgotten about her; she feels abandoned, lonely, and neglected. Like many individuals, it is not easy for her to attribute these personal constraints, and give these nonproductive accessories, totally and completely to the Lord. She, like you, cannot hold back like the squirrel that buries nuts in some locations and begins digging them up only to replant them a few yards away. Or perhaps, like the turtle, which draws its head instantly into its shell when it senses danger or hears a roar of thunder, it becomes motionless with fear. Or like a friend of mine, now deceased, who wondered all of her life about the identity of her father. She thought she bore his last name, but there is no evidence, as neither she nor her mom had the same last name. The assumption was that the mom was married because her name was different, but there was no legal evidence; it could have been her maiden name. The emotional pain in her voice and her thoughts made me feel so sad, so helpless. She frequently verbalized her wish to know who her father was, what he looked like, and whether she shared any physical features with him or her mother. She sometimes felt anger at her mom, which often made her feel frustrated, cried at times, and shared a sense of loneliness and abandonment by her father, and deception by her mom. But then compassion came over her, and she realized she did not know what her mom had been through. As I write this segment, I remember an article I read years earlier. The wishes are so similar, the words so familiar, the pain as deep. A woman standing at her window cried and wished she knew her father. God told her, in a gentle voice, "I am your Father and have always been with you." God provided for both individuals: one survived due to circumstance, and the other, according to the article, was very successful due to lifestyle. These situations remind you that, although you may feel incomplete from a physical perspective, God, through his power, divine love, and providential care, has made you successful in many ways. He has always been there to strengthen, guide, and direct you through difficult times.

Accessorization

As you journey, you must learn to fear the Lord and learn of his incredible power, strength, judgment, forgiving nature, promises, and favor. Learn of his grace, bountiful mercy, and how he provides for each of you during difficult and good times, to learn his expectations for obedience and love. However, you must also understand that disobedience has consequences, and some of them can be life-altering. Know that he gives each believer a suit of armor fitted for each battle. Those pieces of armor, when worn correctly, can help you cope in this world filled with people trying to do you in (Eph 6:10). You should know that this armor is not penetrable. You must understand the requirements for wearing it so that it remains operable, and you can stand the schemes of the devil and evil principalities that have arisen in the last few days.

You must know that God loves you so much that this perfect suit of armor has been woven to prevent fiery darts from entering your very being. God is such a loving Father that he gives all believers a source and arsenal to help fight those evil constraints. These harmful accessories are designed to confuse, keep you weary, and have a heavy burden like a backpack full of rocks, bearing the weight down with so much suffering that you feel locked in, surrounded by a mirror of emotions that lead to suffering from depression and other psychological issues. You can quickly turn to Ephesians chapter 6, beginning at verse 10, and learn about this spiritual arsenal and how to utilize its components daily. Have you unburied yourself for a moment and tried on the suit? It comes in one size that fits all. You must familiarize yourself with each accessory to understand its proper usage and how each piece assists you. Do you keep the arsenal close and have a sense of its spiritual connection to God, guided by the aid of the Holy Spirit, or are you so immersed in life's challenges that you have forgotten about this gift?

The Holy Bible contains the spiritual arsenal and answers to all life circumstances. You will only know its power if you read it. You must be suited for battle, energized with grit and grace to withstand the devil's schemes. As a believer, you must understand that your struggles, feelings of defeat, and anguish are not the result of flesh and blood but of wrestling against the power of this dark

Accessorizing Your Christian Character and Self-Absorbed Nature

world and the uncanny forces of "the evil in the heavenly realms." You must stand still and be firm in your faith while putting on your spiritual armor.

The belt of truth and the breastplate of righteousness allow you to have your feet fitted with the readiness from the gospel of peace. You will take the shield of faith with confidence, which gives you the spiritual ability to extinguish all flaming arrows of the evil one. You will take the helmet of salvation, given to you freely to protect and deliver you from harm, and proudly wear and use the sword of the Spirit, which is the word of God, to avail yourself of knowledge and understanding of his word. Finally, fit yourself with the last piece of the arsenal: pray in the Spirit on all occasions with all kinds of prayers and requests.

After you are familiar with the accessories, you must be alert and vigilant like Nehemiah; you are now ready for a spiritual battle with the Commander-in-Chief on your side. Continue praying for yourself, all believers, and those who do not know God's goodness. With these accessories in your possession, continue to pray and know that God hears your cry; he hears and understands your inarticulate groans, and he is right there with you. The evidence will be miraculous, and there will be a quieting of spirit, a change in your circumstances, a restoration of your joy, and a lessening of your distress, pain, sorrows, and frustration—these change-altering factors, all of which could have been caused by your disobedience to God's expectations or by the enemy trying to confuse and throw you off course. God hears your cry and will not allow you to continue in your self-dug pit of despair and bondage. Remember Daniel in the lion's den, who leaned and depended on God to see him through; the three Hebrew boys in the fiery furnace; or the story of Paul and Silas. God is always present; he is just waiting to hear from you.

The message is that sinners' victories are temporary, alluding to the fact that the person has won and is in control. Look how much God loves you; he gave his only Son, Jesus, who rode a donkey on palm branches, being cheered by a crowd, and a few days later, some of those same people were yelling for him to be crucified. He was arrested, put on trial, found guilty, humiliated, and abused; a crown of thorns was pressed into his head, and blood ran down. He was made to carry a heavy cross up to Calvary; along the way, a man of color had compassion and helped him with that heavy load. He was stretched on that same rugged cross; spikes were driven into his feet and nails in his hands; he was pierced in his side, and water and blood rained out of him; he thirsted and was given vinegar to drink. What an ordeal. He cried out to his Father! Can you hear him calling his Father, and do you recall what he did from the cross that is sometimes so difficult for you, as believers, to do? Jesus said, "Father, forgive them, for they know not what they do." What a marvelous role model. Can you, as a believer, a follower of Christ, forgive those who have bruised and injured you from an emotional perspective? How deep is your faith? Does that hope, faith, and trust still lie within? Is your soul deeply anchored?

4. Sin! Does It Have a Special Wing in Your Heart?

A good man brings good things out of the good stored up in his heart, and an evil man brings evil things out of the evil stored up in his heart. For out of the mouth speaks what the heart is full of.
Luke 6:45 NIV

Hide your face from my sins and blot out all my iniquity. Create in me a pure heart, O God, and renew a steadfast spirit within me.
Ps 51:9–10

Your sinful heart spoils your temple and makes you less pleasing in the sight of God. Your heart must be cleansed from sin through the blood of Jesus Christ. Does your accessorization store ingredients for trouble in your spiritual shelter, body, or temple of God, where the Holy Spirit dwells? Did you carelessly store flammable and nonflammable material in the same area? Have you allowed life's challenges to create a unique, nonproductive wing in your heart?

Accessorizing Your Christian Character and Self-Absorbed Nature

Where are you? Is your heart harboring particles that may ignite fleshly thoughts, such as anger, hate, jealousy, spite, or guilt, or even lead to a fleshly act? Is your heart being formed and worn by dark lines from storing pain of unforgiveness or prideful thoughts? Is your heart hardened by consistent disobedience, making it impossible to feel God's Spirit? Which particles impact your relationship and fellowship (*koinonia*) with God? How can your heart be pure or represent all the spiritual accessories required, such as love, joy, and peace, or be one of God's chambers if it is clouded by negativity and evil? Remember, goodness can't dwell in the same chamber as evil. Perhaps your heart is like a boiler (furnace) or water heater that you forgot to service, and you want to ensure it is free of any deficiencies before use. Is there pain from hurt and despair from life's daily circumstances? Is it possible to minimize risk and implement safety precautions to prevent slippage? These safety precautions should be prayer, fasting, meditation, forgiveness, and Scripture. There is a three-foot rule for fire prevention in the storage area with the water heater or boiler. Is there a three-foot rule with your heart, soul, and mind? These three intersect at a crucial point; however, as with a boiler or water heater, you may have created a severe problem if flammables are stored too close. Did you cause the same catastrophe in your spiritual temple? Did you forget to store wisely or accessorize with coordination in mind? You must avoid storing trouble and give all those igneous thoughts to the Lord. Learn to keep things apart that, when mixed or merged, may cause contentious fumes or draw negative vibes. Are you storing flammables in your spirit, leaving you vulnerable and limiting your spiritual growth?

God expects you to avoid dealing with or having a spirit that has no place in the body of Christ. As a believer, you must prevent the hazardous storing of harmful ingredients that contaminate the inner walls of your very being. You must pray and ask God to help you intentionally accessorize yourself, both internally and externally. You must ask him to help you remove those controllable ingredients, as Paul noted in Gal 5, that may ruin your soul if not contained. In your physical life, you are taught that flammable

Accessorization

materials should not be stored in your garage, basement, or storage shed. Do you take the same precautions for your inner being? Are you as considerate about what is stored in your heart, mind, soul, and very being? Are you careful about your flammables and how you store them to prevent one from igniting another and causing a full eruption that is not in your best interest? What ingredients mix, or what temperature changes trigger them if an eruption occurs? Similar to a volcano, pressure builds over time and becomes intense until the cap gives way, releasing lava filled with melted particles. Fire then rolls down the hill, wiping away everything in its path. There is total devastation and destruction; however, in the future, vegetation and life begin to flourish from the volcanic ash. Is this similar to your eruption? Did you completely transform from the world and its pleasures when you gave your hand to the pastor and your heart to the Lord? Or did you make a partial transformation, continuing to adore the pleasures of the world? Reflecting on Lot's wife, we see that disobedience is life-altering. The heart can be a deceitful and misleading organ.

Where is your spiritual circuit breaker? Your spiritual safety switch works like the electrical system in your home, alerting you when a fault is detected. There is an overload, an overwhelming of your emotional circuit, a risk of emotional breakdown, and severe damage is about to occur. Where is your trip switch? There is a need to interrupt your anxiety and your temperament, and a need to know what tripped your spirituality. Like the circuit breaker in your home, you need to know what caused the interruption so that it does not recur. At home, you hit the appropriate breaker, which resets and reconnects the circuit. God is there, and he is not like a fuse box; he does not need replacing or resetting. He is the Main Circuit Breaker, controlling the entire system from beginning to end. All you need to do is follow his instructions: start with repentance, then initiate obedience to redirect your spiritual current to the right source.

As homeowners, you are careful about plugging in the correct wattage, avoiding circuit overloading, and using extension cords only in certain situations. In a seemingly indistinguishable situation, why do you not treat your inner being equally if you live in a temple not made by human hands? Live smart so your life can be an example for others. Be aware of leaks in your home and spiritual walls that, if left unattended, can cause further destruction. As a believer, you must ensure that your foundation is solid and that you are connected to the Main Circuit Breaker. Through prayer, studying God's word, and learning various spiritual disciplines, you can help build a strong foundation. These are just a few spiritual maintenance tasks you routinely perform to ensure there is no leakage or overload. As a believer, you must continue to pray and seek God's anointing so that he will help upgrade your spiritual system.

Are you storing accessories that may cause trouble in your spiritual self? Anger, hatred, and a lack of forgiveness are but a few accessories that may be hidden in your spiritual self. Your sinful heart is what defiles you. Your heart must be cleansed from your iniquities through the blood of Jesus Christ. What comes from your heart and mind ultimately determines your actions, behavior, and attitude. You must focus on God's words and his expectations, and standards for believers, not on what your peers do or say, but on what you must do. It is challenging for you to walk away from peer pressure. You sometimes feel guilty about abandoning your friends. People may refer to you with degrading names or question your ethnicity or status as an American, as occurred with former President Barack Obama or with the former candidates. Sometimes, people may have difficulty understanding your ethnicity and how an individual can be both Asian American and Black at the same time. Sadly, this happens when people don't expose themselves to other cultures. What will you do? Is your spiritual self strong enough to turn the other cheek? Here is how, as a believer, you can rid yourself of these unwarranted risks that may raise doubts and lead to failure. Issues such as anger and humiliation occur in your daily life. Sometimes, you are the initiator, while at other times, it may be someone else or the enemy setting you up for a test to see if you are all you claim to be. Or perhaps God is placing you in a position to assess your faith and evaluate

Accessorization

your resiliency, courage, trust, and human compassion in preparation for your elevation to a higher calling in him. These harmful accessories are responsible for some of the frustration and spiritual injuries you suffer, such as depression and physical and medical damage caused by bodily ailments each day. When damaging your spiritual self, you must maintain a relationship with God. He gives you directions or instructions to help you remain firm in his word. His word tells you how to rid yourself of these strongholds and maintain yourself to remain whole or regain wholeness and oneness in Christ. These burden downers help you grow and strengthen your faith by deepening your understanding of how being with God fosters regulation in prayer and service.

"Studying the word give believers authority for authentic discipleship because God gave believers his word for guidance and spiritual growth."[20] Life is so concise. Nothing is promised to anyone. Your eternity with God and your relationship with him may be in jeopardy. You must think before acting or speaking. Please think of the consequences of your actions. Don't allow the power of your position and the deep need for public recognition put you in jeopardy of God's gift of eternal life. Remember, your actions have serious consequences that may ignite a reaction and turn into a life-altering situation. God further expects his children to continue to accessorize their spiritual being by implementing and understanding the following accessories in their daily lives. While these appear simplistic, resisting is often challenging if you are not grounded in God's word and teachings.

GOD'S EXPECTATIONS FOR HIS CHILDREN

1. **Resist Temptation.** In Scripture, temptation is simply a test or a trial, either by God or Satan, that provides an opportunity for believers to choose between faithfulness and unfaithfulness to God. Satan enticed Jesus after he had been in the desert fasting for forty days and nights. Knowing and thinking that Jesus was weak and vulnerable, Satan tried

---

20. Turner, *Biblical Theology*, 99.

with his cunning voice to get Jesus to turn stones into bread, throw himself off the mountain, or offer Jesus the world and all its splendor. When none of the temptations worked, Satan left Jesus, and angels came to minister to him (Matt 4:1–11). Could you withstand these temptations? Jesus was weak and hungry, but God provided for him. God will do the same for you if you trust and obey his will and accept his way. James 1:8 describes the double-minded man, who is unstable in all his ways, while Heb 4:2 (NIV) tells you that God does not expect you to cause another to stumble. Be courageous and strong, endure the hardship as Jesus did, and watch God's salvation at work. This courage in your actions is essential to your salvation as you contemplate accessorization; remember that God tells you in 1 Cor 16:13 (NIV) to "be on guard" and "stand firm in the faith." You may find yourself standing alone with Jesus as your anchor. God uses trials and tribulations to see if you are truly committed to him and trust in his word, having faith in him, or will you break like a dried twig in the desert sun? At the same time, God tests you as well, to make you stronger and draw you closer to him. Satan uses every opportunity to place temptations in your path, causing you to fall. Can you withstand the test? Can you endure hardships? Are you deeply rooted in the Lord?

2. **Being Courageous and Forthright.** It takes a special kind of person to know how to accessorize their attitude so they can be a positive force in others' lives, even to the point of sacrificing their own life to save others from harm. Reflecting on the Bible, Esther is an empowering force. Following Mordecai's instructions, she did not reveal her nationality and family background (Esth 2: 10–11 NIV). She groomed herself in God's word to face the challenge with steadfastness, perseverance, and courage. Through God's providential care, she was instrumental in saving her people from extermination. Hers was a divine assignment and a test of character; her personal life, as the new queen, was placed on hold so that she could follow God's instructions and be obedient to

Accessorization

his will. God expects you to be mature in his word so that you do not allow yourself to be taken back by desires and deceit. A good example of this is Lot's wife, who, when God told the family to leave Sodom and Gomorrah and instructed them not to look back or they would turn to pillars of salt, Lot's wife did just the opposite. Her disobedience and self-will had life-altering consequences; when she looked back, she was turned into a pillar of salt. Imagine the impact on Lot and his family. There was absolutely nothing he could do; she had failed to follow instructions, she was disobedient, and she suffered the punishment of eternal death.

When you allow yourself to become engulfed unthinkingly in the lives of others, you will fall short of God's glory. You may find yourself encumbered in a false world, locked away with people who, through no fault of their own, are cast off to spend the rest of their lives with their minds and emotions locked in a world, sadly, of no return. When their minds are restored, they look up from the bottomless pit to slowly fall deeper and deeper into non-reality. You realize through your despair that you must reach up, grasp a straw of hope, and see a faint ray of sunlight through the dark cloud. You know you must fight; you must have courage; your thoughts must be honest with yourself, directed toward truth and reality. It will be painful to face the truth; it may set you back, but painfully, you have lived in doubt and your belief. Reality struck, and what you thought was hope, for a time, was like dust blown away by a strong and different wind. You may ask yourself, "Where did the time go?" Why did you not see, or understand? . . . You must fight to bring yourself to the brink of the top and keep climbing. This is the hope, the size of a mustard seed, needed to get you back to God's divine will, his purpose for your life, and his specific assignment for you to carry forth (Matt 13:31–32). Many hymns and spirituals were written to give believers hope, strengthen, inspire, and deepen their faith in God. As you reflect on some of these hymns and spirituals, is your soul anchored and built on a solid rock? Times will become challenging. Will your

Accessorizing Your Christian Character and Self-Absorbed Nature

anchor hold? As the waves challenge and confront you, is your anchor secured?

3. **Be Humble.** God expects you to learn to wait and trust in him. Waiting increases patience and humility if you have hope and faith in God. In Isa 40:31 (NIV), believers are told, "But they that wait upon the Lord shall renew their strength, they shall mount up with wings as eagles; they shall run, and not be weary; and they shall walk, and not faint." Waiting is something that some believers have not learned to do. They want it, whatever it is, now. Where is your humility? God states in 2 Chr 7:14 (NLT) what you need to do, yet you fall short; you are not listening; sometimes, he might shut up heaven so it does not rain. You have experienced months without rain or flooding, hurricanes with massive destruction, and loss of life because you sometimes fail to follow the instructions and directions of emergency procedures. God clearly states in verse 14 the humility he expects, and when that humility is honored, "then if my people who are called by my name will humble themselves and pray and seek my face and turn from their wicked ways, I will forgive their sins and restore their land." God is seeking your humility and obedience. In 2025, with so many signs that the end of time is near, man continues to sin and, in some respect, is disobedient and self-willed as God's chosen people were. You remain revengeful and sinful, believing that you are self-sufficient, self-made, self-reliant, self-willed, and you are not dependent on God. It appears some people have become self-directed and believe that humanity can set itself up as a god and do as it will. The most outstanding example of humility is Jesus Christ; he did nothing for himself or by himself, being dependent and obedient to his Father. What is humility? Stated in Prov 22:4, humility is "the fear of the Lord; its wages are riches and honor and life." Are you humble? What accessories show that you have humility? David tells believers in 1 Chr 29:11–12 that all we have comes from God, and it is simply on loan from God. Believers, we own nothing on this earth. It is all provided to

Accessorization

and for us by a divine and loving Father. You must manage it well. Look at the world today; how much of what is occurring is the product of disobedience, greed, single-mindedness, and excessive pride flowing from an unrenewed heart and a boastful, retributive spirit of self?

4. **Be Grateful.** Enjoy the "seat" at the table (John 10:1–5). God expects you not to allow evil thoughts to enter your heart against another brother or sister. He expects you to be more Christlike. The seat at the table has been prepared primarily for you. The table overflows with love and generosity because of who you serve and your deep, abiding faith in him. It is adorned with the gift of God, which strengthens your walk and encourages you to keep going. At the table, your cup overflows with goodness and mercy. In the Twenty-Third Psalm, the Lord is your Shepherd, which means he watches over you, guides and directs your path, and provides, protects, and keeps you together under his watchful eyes and mighty wings. Please take a moment, close your eyes, and envision the table your Shepherd prepares in the presence of those who may set stumbling blocks before you. Imagine what they must think when they see the bountiful table he has prepared before you, with new mercies, filled with new blessings, and special favors every day. Hear the quiet stream that flows daily, providing calm waters to quench your spiritual thirst and calm your racing thoughts. But you must be humble. You must learn to express gratitude to God for all he has done; being grateful, thankful, and appreciative from the heart represents a genuine, authentic sincerity.

5. **Gird Yourself in the Armor of God** (Eph 6:10 NIV). When you drape yourself in the whole armor of God, delight in God's trust, and have faith the size of a mustard seed, you are shielded from the wiles of night. However, your draping does not eliminate the fact that things or events will occur that will not deter you, which will cause doubt. Do not allow yourself to be taken off course; stay on your pathway. This may test

Accessorizing Your Christian Character and Self-Absorbed Nature

your faith, commitment, and trust in God. You may have been on this battlefield for a long time; have you learned to gird up for spiritual warfare? Have you tried the war suit that is fitted for any spiritual battle? If not, have you inspected it lately? Does it still hold fast for you in the twenty-first century, amid lies and deceit, the cunningness of the devil that seems to impart man's heart, mind, and soul? This suit can protect you from the evil that confronts you and tries to derail you. Here are the components of your spiritual suit already designed and equipped by the Master Seamster and completely accessorized with all the necessary items for warfare. You protect your head, heart, and hands when you accessorize with the armor. As a believer, you are guided in your footsteps and, when the load becomes unbearable, look at your silhouette; you are being carried over the rough mountains of life. Sometimes it seems like God is so far away because the pain is so great, but then a small voice reminds you he is still there. The believer's attire is not just a suit, but a spiritual armor God bestows. These armor pieces are not mere accessories but are essential tools that enable you to withstand the attacks of evil forces. God provides you with a source to help you fight those constraints that keep you confined and weary. With the tools of this arsenal below, you know you must pray, continue in the field, and follow God's instructions for obedience as one of his believers. You must understand that God hears your cry, and you know he does. Remember, he knew you when you were formed within your mother's body. The evidence must be miraculous, and quiet Spirit (a feeling of inner peace, a sense of calmness, deep serenity), a change, a restoration, your distress and pain, and sorrows and frustrations will no longer keep you in the pit of despair and bondage. Remember that we are all unique and at various stages in our spiritual growth and development. For some of us, change may be immediate, while for others, it may be long-term; however, regardless of the time frame, change will come. So be encouraged; remain faithful; God knows you from within.

Accessorization

THE PIECES OF THE ARMOR ARE:

a) The first piece of armor for the wearer is the Belt of Truth, which girt your loins with truth. A belt usually holds things up, keeping them organized, preventing them from falling, and maintaining things in the preferred order. The Belt of Truth, buckled around the wearer's waist, comes from God because you can't muster your own truth. Like a strap around the wearer's waist, the belt of truth is designed to encircle the wearer. It protects and keeps them safe from their enemy, and each holds God's word sacred. How is your lifestyle? It does not need to be perfect, but is it at a point that God can find some righteous living? Is the belt ready to secure the first armor of truth? Are you prepared and protected by God's word? Can you resist the enticements of temptations, lies, and numerous falsehoods that may confront you as a believer? Is the belt fitting properly around your waist, or is it bulging with tension from disobedience?

b) The second piece of armor in the soldier's left hand is the Breastplate of Righteousness, which prevents God's children from succumbing to the fatal attack from the enemy. This attack may be deadly if the wearer falls into sins, such as succumbing to spiritual forces, bitterness, anger, and other devilish schemes. "If we do not protect ourselves with righteousness, we open ourselves up to attack from the enemy and can fall into sin."[21] Through Jesus Christ, God's mercy and compassion provide forgiveness of your sins and iniquities, made possible by Christ, who shed his blood at Calvary for the remission of your sins (Eph 6:14). According to Benware, "Righteousness has its source in God himself and does not come by human effort. It comes by faith."[22] (Rom 3:21-22) In Exod 28, the breastplate was worn over a priestly garment, symbolizing divine judgment and revolutions. As believers, your lives are confronted by temptations on a daily

---

21. Abraham, "Weekly Devotional."
22. Benware, Survey of the Old Testament, 212.

basis; therefore, James encourages you to "submit yourselves to God." The breastplate was adorned with twelve precious gemstones, each representing one of the twelve tribes of Israel. There was no need for armor to cover the soldier's back; his role was to advance the unit and spread the word of God. To do this, the believer will confront spiritual adversaries head-on. Therefore, as a believer, you must be ready for spiritual battle. God has your back; he is ever-present. You are in a spiritual battle. Are you ready?

c) The third piece of armor fits your feet with the readiness provided by the Shoes of the Gospel of Peace, which allows you to share God with others with unwavering commitment at all times. As you are told in Matt 28:19, "All power is given unto me in heaven and earth. We are therefore to go and teach all nations, baptizing them in the name of the Father; and of the Son, and the Holy Ghost: teaching them to observe all things whatsoever I have commanded you: and, lo, I am with you always, even unto the end of the world." Amen. This is a command to believers as well as an expectation for them. God endows and blesses each of you with a spiritual gift, and some believers with more than one gift, and expects you to help those who do not know or have not experienced him become disciples of him. These gifts are designed to edify and build up the body of Christ. The gifts are not intended for personal gratification or to be stored away like precious diamonds; instead, they are meant to help disciples grow and become part of kingdom-building.

d) The fourth piece of armor on the suit is the Shield of Faith, known as *"thureos"* in Greek.[23] In Scripture, the Shield of Faith can guard you during trials like a shield protects the warrior in battle. The Shield of Faith gives you divine protection and the spiritual ability to extinguish all the flaming arrows of the evil one (Eph 6:16). As a believer, you rely on your faith and trust in Almighty God to face daily challenges in your home or faith community. Psalm 119:114 reminds

23. Bible Hub, "2375 thureos" Shield of Faith.

Accessorization

you that God is your refuge and shield; you must put your hope in God's word. Christ is your shield.

e) The fifth piece of armor is the Helmet of Salvation. This protective helmet ensures that your thoughts are pure, tempered, and shielded from sinfulness that may penetrate your hearts, leading to a fall from grace. It helps you discern what is good, pure, and true in God's eyes, guiding you to think spiritually rather than fleshly. The Helmet of Salvation shields God's children from "all that is unnatural, impure, untrue, and unnecessary, providing a sense of security" (Eph 6:17 NIV).

You are his children (John 1:12–13 NIV), and you are reborn not of a physical birth resulting from human passion or plans, but a birth from God. It is further stated in Isa 59:17 that he put on righteousness as a breastplate and the Helmet of Salvation upon his head, and put on the garments himself of vengeance for clothing, and was clad with zeal as a cloak. This highlights the spiritual significance of the helmet as a symbol of protection, guarding, shielding, and keeping God's children under his care. You know that arrows and other obstacles can hit the helmet, but the helmet remains impenetrable.

f) The sixth piece of armor is the Sword of the Spirit, held in the wearer's right hand. This powerful, accessorized element represents God's word, equipping and protecting you against the enemy. Scripture tells you about the two-edged sword with two sharp edges and corrective and penetrating powers against evil and evildoers. In essence, it is noted that there are both "good and bad parts." The Sword is a weapon used in spiritual warfare to fight off the enemy, and its purpose is the same. Daniel McCoy notes that the "Sword of the Spirit is God's way of putting Satan on the defensive."[24] It is the primary defensive weapon, a powerful armor designed to be used against your enemy in the carnal world. The sword is a weapon against spiritual forces and attacks on the word of God, giving believers the ability and courage to combat evil with truth and confidence. God gives believers in Scripture

---

24. McCoy, Sword of the Spirit.

Accessorizing Your Christian Character and Self-Absorbed Nature

the authority to be prepared for the battlefield, which is constant in their daily lives. Today, the forces have become so prevalent, bold, and daring that they claim power over God's people. However, as believers, you must remember that God has equipped you with a full arsenal: one piece of defensive armor and six pieces of offensive armor. All you need to do is learn to use them with the power of the Holy Spirit. If you recall the conflict between David and Saul, the priest instructed David to use Goliath's sword. While it was mighty, it did not compare to God's word (Heb 4:12). It states, "For the word of God is quick, and powerful, and sharper than any two-edged sword, piercing even to the dividing asunder of soul and spirit, and of the joint and marrow, and is a discerner of the thoughts and intents of the heart." In other words, while the sword is mighty and powerful, capable of killing with a single blow, it is not as powerful or piercing as God's word. In addition, the word of God exposes, corrects, rebukes, pronounces judgment, brings light to darkness, breaks chains of spiritual bondage, and shows you the way to salvation (1 Pet 1:23). The mighty strike of the sword ends human life, but the mighty strike of God's word gives spiritual and divine substance to the soul of man. You must keep in mind that in 2025, believers are in a spiritual war. If you look at some people in leadership positions, you wonder how they can do and say some things you have witnessed. There appears to be no empathy, no regard for human life, a coldness, and unyieldingness; and definitely, there seems to be no regard for the rule of law. People are treated as if they are less than human. As I reflect on so many things that have occurred since January 20, 2025, my one thought is . . . "But God, who sits high and looks low, will cast judgment in due time."

g) The seventh and final piece of armor is Prayer. Prayer must be done with a humble spirit, without doubt, and without an ulterior motive. Prayer is the believer's way of communicating with God. While God sees, knows, and hears everything about you, prayer is a humbling way to trust and depend

Accessorization

totally on him. And let us, as believers, pray and pray in the Spirit on all occasions, fervently with all kinds of prayers and requests. With the picture and factual knowledge in your mind, be alert, be on guard, and be suited for the battle that is about to begin. Keep on praying not just for yourself but for all of God's children. Continue to pray, even when it seems like there is no answer, even when you are at your lowest, even when the whole mountain is caving in on you; pray.

The message implied by the armor is that sinners' victories are temporary, giving troubled believers the illusion that the victor is in control. Learn how God loves you; he loved you so much he gave his Son, Jesus, who, during the week of Palm Sunday, rode over beautiful palms to be falsely accused eventually; he was tortured, and a crown of thorns was placed on and pressed into his head until blood ran down his face; he was judged by a court of his peers who found him guilty; and the final cry was to crucify him there on Calvary's cross. To further humiliate him, they strategically placed him between two thieves, his hands and feet pierced with nails. He was pierced in his side until blood and water ran down. He thirsted like any human being going through torture by angry men who whipped him all night long, and then, to add to the severity of his punishment, he was made to carry a heavy wooden cross with the assistance of a Black man who felt compassion for him and tried to share his physical load. The spiritual load of the sin of mankind, which began with disobedience in Eden, could only be carried by Jesus. Jesus asked for a simple drink of water to quench his thirst, but instead he was given vinegar-soaked on a rag. Can you close your eyes and eliminate background noise so you can listen quietly as he calls out to his Father? Can you hear him calling his Father sometimes for a sense of relief from the agony and weight of human sin and a feeling that he had been abandoned during his darkest hour? Do you recall what he did there from the cross?

During all his suffering and knowing what was before him, he remained obedient to his Father, and was compassionate enough to say, "Father, please forgive them, for they know not what they

Accessorizing Your Christian Character and Self-Absorbed Nature

do." Could you be so compassionate? Could you seek forgiveness for someone inflicting pain on you just because you are different in your ways, in your beliefs, and in your national origin? Jesus could have said no to his Father, but he did not. Could you have been so kind, so lenient, so forgiving? He sacrificed his life willingly so you, disobedient and non-forgiving people, could have eternal life. What a cost! What a price to pay! What love, given willingly. Scripture tells us that he was buried in a borrowed tomb because he would not be interred for long. On the third day, he arose from the grave, descended into the pit of hell, and ascended into heaven. What a glorious, unselfish act of Jesus. This is good news! While Jesus died for each of you and you have an opportunity to repent of your wickedness, some of you are disillusioned by wicked people who will do anything to get ahead. As a believer, you become stuck. How can some people be so cunning, careless, deceitful, and underhanded, and say whatever they want about another person, with seemingly no repercussions for their behavior? You often see this on television or in virtual media, or you have personal knowledge of people who believe that the foundation laid by the court system or written into the Constitution applies only to a particular class of people. It is so painful and disturbing to hear what they appear to get away with; it sometimes shakes my faith. This thinking, however, is meaningless; their reward is temporal. While they believe they have won, have the upper hand, and are sailing through a sea of crystal blue water under a clear sky, they don't understand God's will for obedience. The sea will become turbulent; the waters will rise and move over them, as seen with Hurricanes Helene and Milton in 2024, causing widespread destruction and life-altering effects. This, too, may have been initiated by severe climate change, which some in power refuse to accept because the necessary environmental changes could affect their status and wealth. These individuals must seek repentance and learn to trust and depend on God. He allows you to express your grief to him, and because you can bring everything to him in prayer, you find abundant joy, hope, and peace amid sorrow and pain. The challenge is manageable when God intercedes, and there is evidence of

Accessorization

change. Thank God for proof of his love, compassion, and mercy, which he gives you new every day. You hear your children's cries and provide for them. "For in peace I will lie down and sleep, for you and you alone, O Lord, will keep me safe." You know you are a sheep, and he will provide for your safety and security, because he is the Great Shepherd.

He then asked the question. How bright is your light? Is it strong enough and guided by the Holy Spirit to ward off those attitudes, emotions, and behaviors that cause you to lose sight and favor with God?

June Masters Bacher shares that today, we live in a world of darkness in which even our secular problem-solving are beginning to stumble. In spite of our "social conscious" all around us is evidence of ignorance, illiteracy, and dark imagining. As believers, we can add additional accessories that may be stumbling blocks to include: bitterness, hate, jealousy, anger, frustration, lies, greed, graft, and a desire to elevate oneself to a position that allows one to control those who live in a free democracy.[25]

Romans 2:19 tells you that you are "a light for those in the dark," a light to help them find their way through the darkness of time and their troubled soul. The world is so big, and your light is so tiny; how can you break through the darkness? Each of you is a star in God's world, a light that can break through the hardness of hearts and a lamp that provides guided light to show the way to those who have fallen off the straight and narrow path. Suppose you, regardless of your socioeconomic status, educational background, or political affiliation, combine all your lights. In that case, you can break through the thick night that seems to engulf your every being. Like God's heaven, a star is never missing; each tiny light twinkles until dawn. Like the stars in God's heaven, they twinkle even though you can't see them on a cloudy night. Let your light shine so that others may see its beam and follow.

Believers face daily challenges as men, fathers, women, wives, mothers, role models, and leaders in their churches. Expectations can sometimes be overwhelming, and your roles are constantly

25. Bacher, *Where Are the Lamps*, cited in *Women's Devotional Bible*, 1121.

Accessorizing Your Christian Character and Self-Absorbed Nature

tested and confronted each day by various factors or individuals. Yet you are expected to excel and do so with a smile, even when your heart aches, your body is weary from the day's toil, you are emotionally drained, and your arms feel heavy—sometimes too tired to hold up the lamp so others can find their way. You think you cannot take another step, but God hears your secret prayers or groans and gives you the strength to move forward. How do you move forward? In his name and under his divine power and providential care. He soothes your doubts, fears, and pain, whispering gently, telling you to go on. You move forward by working together, putting together each light to make the world a better and brighter place. How do you begin? It all starts with the prayer often attributed to Michelangelo: "God, grant me desire to be more than I can ever accomplish."

Have you considered the brightness of your light for each of you who will take the time to read my book on accessorization? Don't be like the five foolish bridesmaids. I urge you to light your lamp regardless of the circumstances. Trim your wick, clean the globe, and let God's power, grace, and favor guide you in a new direction. If you meet someone at the crossroads of their life, what do you do, and how do you aid this brother or sister? Try putting on a bright face, even if you don't feel like it. You are a people of grace, chosen by God to be a beacon of hope for the weary, the lost, the forsaken, and the downtrodden. Is your beam bright enough for them to see and follow? Don't let your globe become cloudy due to the aforementioned elements.

Remember, Jesus, surrounded by endless requests and weary from walking many miles, saw the burden another carried and offered to help with the load. When you are wearied, worn, and tired and have trouble keeping the light burning, do as Jesus did by asking a simple question: "What can I do for you?" Who knows what these words can do for another or you? I asked each reader, "How bright is your light?" Can another see its beam through the darkness? Has it been cleansed from sin through the blood of your Lord and Savior, Jesus?

3

The Spiritual Ingredient Mix for Accessorizing Your Temple

Therefore, as God's chosen people, holy and dearly loved, clothe yourselves with compassion, kindness, humility, gentleness, and patience. Bear with each other and forgive your grievances against one another. Forgive as the Lord forgave you. All these virtues put in love bind them all together in perfect unity. Let the peace of Christ rule in your heart since, as members of one body, you were called to peace. And be thankful.

COL 3:12–15 NIV

USING SPIRITUAL INGREDIENTS AS accessories helps you discern proper and unethical behavior, emotions, and manners. It prevents you from justifying your sinful ways and nature by quoting Scriptures, showing that you are correct and that God will forgive you. You must understand that you are change agents for Christ. In 1 Thess 5:8, it is written, "But let us who are of the day be sober, putting on the breastplate of faith, and love; and for a helmet, the hope of salvation." The ingredients embedded in this passage of

The Spiritual Ingredient Mix for Accessorizing Your Temple

Scripture are sobriety, faith, love, the helmet, the hope of salvation, and holding fast to things deemed reasonable. To accessorize your temple and make it a place where God can use you, you must seek God's help in discerning his will and expectations. Whatever you need as believers to enhance your lives, such as seeking wisdom, you should ask God, who generously provides this ingredient without holding anything against you. You are instructed that once you ask, you must have faith and believe he will give it to you. Sometimes, human nature or the flesh blocks you from receiving what God has in store for you, and when you doubt God's goodness, James says, "We are double-minded and are unstable in all we do" (Jas 1:8) You must understand the constant war between the flesh and the Spirit (Heb 12:10). You must learn to discover the many spiritual benefits of living and engaging in the life plan God gave you, which began to disintegrate due to disobedience in the garden of Eden. Still, through God's grace, favor, and mercy, he gave you an opportunity for declaration of justification through faith in Christ when he freed you from the penalty for your sins (Rom 3:24). The Holy Spirit dwells within you to assist you with the ongoing process of sanctification. This is warranted because of your sins and unwillingness to follow and be obedient to God's instructions. The Spirit helps you become more like Christ, and remain in his image (Rom 6:19 NLT). Another benefit of God's plan for your life is purification, the process of being cleansed from your iniquities and transgressions. Through the precious blood of the Lamb, offered as a perfect sacrifice for your sins, God seeks to purify you, wash you clean, and make you spotless (Heb 9:14 NLT). And the final state for your life is glorification. You have attained perfection and eternal life with God through the death, burial, and resurrection of his Son, Jesus. This salvation encompasses all of these attributes, securing your deliverance from sin and life-altering consequences. In the book of Philippians 3:21 (NLT), following his instructions and precepts allows you to enjoy a beautiful home in glory with the promised streets of gold. Have you purchased the plan? Have you considered the benefits

Accessorization

of becoming a change agent for Christ, utilizing your spiritual wisdom to help others grow and understand the Roman Road to Salvation?

1. Change Agents for Christ

Believers are change agents for Christ, moving forward to make disciples regardless of the circumstances or challenges they face. Ephesians 5:8 tells you that you are a light, and just as the batteries of the light are the source, so is the Vine for believers. You illuminate the accessories of grace, peace, and joy because you are connected to the Light of the world. There are no charges or monthly fees to use the Source. He is available, and God expects you to be sensitive and resist indulging in those worldly accessories that draw you from him, causing your light to become dim and difficult to see clearly.

Change agents are trained. You have specific assignments from God, and you are imitators who strive to live a life of love. As Christ loves you regardless of your imperfections, you must love one another. Ephesians 5:15–18 instructs you to be careful about how you live your life; you must live wisely, cherish every moment, and take advantage of every opportunity because you are a witness, and evil lurks in every corner. As one of Christ's change agents, you are expected to submit to one another out of reverence for Christ. You must repent and hold each other as Christ holds you. Change agents for Christ allow their roots in God to grow deeper in him, grasp on to him, and live lives built on those accessories that strengthen their faith so that they may be firm and steadfast in the faith. Change agents have specific qualities, such as effective communication and the ability to adapt in murky situations. They may be strategic problem-solvers and possess the resilience necessary for outstanding leadership under diverse circumstances. They are creative in building positive and effective trust and establishing rapport with others. These individuals can collaborate under duress, address change with empathy, remain firmly committed to the word of God, and inspire others when they feel overwhelmed.

The Spiritual Ingredient Mix for Accessorizing Your Temple

Change agents are good listeners, possess a nonjudgmental spirit, empathetic, and keep their minds focused on Christ so that nonsense cannot penetrate the three critical essentials of the human being—heart, mind, and spirit. Remember, Christ is the head of every ruler and authority overall (Col 2:12–16).

Christ expects you in the Spirit to think about things pleasing to the Holy Spirit, who dwells in you and serves as your Comforter and Guide (Rom 8:1–10). You are expected to be a positive role model who actively promotes the gospel and makes disciples for Christ, as he instructs you in Matt 28:19–20 "to go."

To conduct and implement this plan of God, you are expected to have the following accessorized characteristics:

a) **Have Confidence in God.** The Hebrew word "*batach*" is often translated as "confidence" in the Bible. It can also mean "trust." Confidence is a firm belief that you can rely on God totally and completely. Unlike you, who change like the weather, God never changes. This gives you a sense of security, knowing that he will never leave or forsake you; he always keeps his promises, his word is truth, and he never goes back on his word. He will only send you out when he has spiritually, emotionally, and physically prepared you for the assignment. In the world, accessories enable you to enhance your personality and add a little "spice" to your look, and when you look great, you become more confident about yourself. This, however, is self-accessorized; it enhances the outer self but leaves the inner self vulnerable to the challenges it brings. Thus, you are assured that the power and grace of God totally and fully keep you; he guides your footsteps and gives you refuge from the storm. David was confident that God would deliver him from the Philistines, just as he had in other circumstances. You, like David, can look back over your life and reflect on the situations God has brought you through; he did not have to do it, but he did. You know and firmly believe with assurance and confidence that your destiny and your

Accessorization

future are secured in God because of your faith and trust in him. Have you accessed the plan?

b) **Develop a Spiritual Habit.** Pray daily, fervently, and without ceasing. In Col 4:2, 5, Paul instructs you to continue in prayer and watch in the same with thanksgiving . . . and in verse 5, he further instructs you to walk in wisdom toward them that are without, redeeming the time. Prayer is like a funnel. It provides a particular passage to God to seek guidance, gather strength, give thanks and adoration, find new meaning, and continue learning more about his deepness. It provides you with the assurance of Calvary and the shedding of his Son's blood for your redemption. It represents how God's love extends itself to your uttermost being. His open arms demonstrate the enormity of his love, goodness, mercy, and kindness. You can communicate with him anywhere, anytime. His door is always open. You lift your eyes to heaven, clasp your hand, and enter into his presence.

Praying hands are shaped somewhat like funnels—narrow and pointed at the top, and as they angle down, they become more expansive, enhancing their appearance. This visual presence gives a sense that you are safe and secure in God's hands. If you have used a funnel to pour liquids, you would have observed the liquid running directly to the very end before spreading throughout the container. A funnel is a tube or pipe that is wide at the top and narrow at the bottom, used for guiding liquid or powder into a small opening.[1] As your prayers go up to heaven, God may send you down blessings too numerous to contain—like the fishermen's net, too small and weak to hold the bounty of fish God provided. Is your funnel open and cleaned to receive God's abundance?

c) **Be Compassionate.** God expects you to be kind to each other. In Gal 5:22, he gives you nine characteristics, known as the fruit of the Spirit, to guide and direct you through daily difficulties and challenges. Utilizing these principles keeps

---

1. Wikipedia, "Funnel."

The Spiritual Ingredient Mix for Accessorizing Your Temple

you close to him. I firmly believe these nine characteristics are significant in each believer's life because the word "fruit" means "the result, product, outcome, or effect produced by the Spirit in the life of each believer." Unlike the gifts of the Spirit, where only one may be given to some believers, all nine characteristics of the fruit of the Spirit are present virtues in the life of each believer. Therefore, the believer's life is accessorized by the nine attributes of the fruit of the Spirit. God has accessorized his children through his unmerited grace and divine mercy with the nine fruit of the Spirit. As long as you desire, you can linger with the Great Shepherd; you need not fear when things become more challenging because he leads you through darkness amid the heavy storm and blistering sun (Ps 121). You don't need to worry whenever you are hungry or in need; he is a God who replenishes and overflows the table, and you never run out of food or favor. As you move through the fruit of the Spirit, you note what God has instructed through his Son, Jesus, the Fruit, to help you meet life's challenges. Throughout the New Testament, Jesus provided guidelines and lessons through parables to help humanity understand his instructions and teachings, avoiding life's pitfalls and temptations. God's expectations and instructions are not new. As previously shared, these instructions and expectations were given to humanity in the garden of Eden. God would have given humanity a life without any worry, free of trials and tribulations, if man had been obedient. However, man's oneness and fellowship with God was severed through selective hearing, the art of free will, and a disobedient and questioning spirit. But a compassionate and merciful Father, through grace and his forgiveness, gave you another opportunity for eternal life through the birth, death, and resurrection of his Son, Jesus. Follow and understand the teachings of Jesus Christ, and follow and understand the characteristics of the fruit of the Spirit. Your path will be more precise, your burdens will be lighter, and

Accessorization

your understanding richer. Each characteristic of the fruit is explicitly laid out for you in Gal 5:22–23.

These are noted and expanded on through life experiences:

1. Love (Greek words for love: *"Agape"*—unconditional or selfless love; *"Eros"*—romantic, passionate love; *"Philia"*—affectionate love in the context of friendship). The first fruit of the Spirit is one of God's commands and expectations for you to love as he loves unconditionally, with no keeping tabs, and deeply rooted in his word. Do you see Jesus? No, but you feel his presence, which surrounds you, indwells you, holds you, and shields you, as you are enfolded within the presence of the Holy Spirit, whose transformative power is in your life. He touches your inner being and helps you love those who spitefully use you, leading you regardless. Love without doubt or finger-pointing. With all the sins you commit each day, sins of omission and commission, God continues to forgive you and continues loving you. He loves you so that he gave his only Son to rescue you from sin and eternal damnation. What love!

    As Scripture states, "God is love." He could have allowed you to go straight to eternal hell following Adam and Eve's disobedience, which altered the lives of all humanity. Nevertheless, his love reached beyond the gates of hell and, through his Son, conquered hell and allowed you to have access to fruitful and eternal life through salvation. In Mark 12:29–30 (NLT), of all the commandments, "Jesus replied, 'The most important commandment is this: "Listen, O Israel! The Lord our God is the one and only Lord. And you must love the Lord your God with all your heart, all your soul, all your mind, and all your strength."'"

2. Joy (the Greek word is *"chara"*) is an enduring attribute of the heart and spirit and a natural part of the believer's faith. When you follow Jesus, you should experience a more profound and richer sense of joy. As Jesus says in John 15:11 (KJV), "These things have I spoken unto you . . . that your joy might be

The Spiritual Ingredient Mix for Accessorizing Your Temple

full." Because of your connectedness to the fruit of the Spirit, you, as a believer, can experience the joy of the Lord, as noted in Scripture, which is your strength. During these turbulent times, it is a joy to read and experience the Lord through his word. All of your joy comes from your personal relationship with God, which is anchored and deeply rooted in your faith and trust in Almighty God. I am reflecting on the serious illness God brought our son, Jeffrey, through, which brings joy and thanksgiving to our hearts, thinking of his goodness, mercy, and his abundant grace and favor, which brings comfort and encouragement.

As a believer, to experience joy in the Lord, you must develop a personal relationship with him and be intentionally consistent in your time with him. Even when you are not consistent, God still blesses you—why not take some time to thank him? In the book of 1 Thessalonians 5:16–18 (NLT), God tells you, "Always be joyful. Never stop praying. Be thankful in all circumstances, for this is God's will for you who belong to Christ Jesus." As a believer, to experience God's joy, you must learn to pray, be ever thankful, and, no matter how small the reason, rejoice and remain in close *koinonia* and relationship with Jesus. Because of the special relationship, your connection to the Vine as a branch gives you the sustainability and strength of the grand live oak tree. It is rooted and grounded, which allows it to bend and sway back and forth in the wind; you need to find yourself like the great oak, rooted deeply in God's word. You may falter under a heavy load, but you can withstand and work through, go around, or over obstacles, challenges, and circumstances planted in your path. You are rooted; remember Job, who overcame through God's power and might.

3. Peace (peace is "*Eirene*" in Greek and "*shalom*" in Hebrew). God tells believers that he gives them peace, and his peace is with them. Romans 5:1 says, "Therefore, since you have been justified through faith, you have peace with God through our Lord Jesus Christ, through whom you have gained access

Accessorization

by faith into this grace in which you now stand." So, you experience the peace of God and the peace with God. When you experience peace, you can reflect on the Twenty-Third Psalm: "The Lord is my Shepherd." You can hear a whisper if you close your eyes and listen to the quiet stream mentioned in the passage of Scripture. The peace of Christ should be evident in your life and rule your life. When you experience God's peace, your mind is at rest. You can sleep without worrying about tomorrow's challenges, avoiding things that frustrate you and cause unnecessary emotional distress. Pray, and leave everything in his hands. It is not easy to let go and let God. You can't see the depths of a situation or focus on your surroundings when your spirit is disturbed and your emotions are uncontained. You are like a mound of red ants, quiet and doing your daily chores until someone disturbs you. You become unraveled, distressed, attacking, and moving in any direction without thought. However, your purpose may be to strike anyone or anything that crosses your path with a venomous sting. When you focus on the Lord and seek his abiding peace, you will experience a sense of serenity, a sense of comfort, a sense of security, and a deep calmness within your soul. God continues to be your safety net; he is your protector. When you experience God, your soul and heart are with him. This means that your thoughts, feelings, and emotions are not within your personal control but are in God's control (Jer 17:9 NIV). Therefore, the heart of a believer is described as deceitful, and this is why God's peace needs to be in control, not your heart. When you experience God's peace, it will exceed anything you can imagine. "His peace will guard your heart and mind, two critical elements of the human body, as you live in Christ Jesus" (Phil 4:7 NLT). Take a deep breath. God's presence has touched you, and your spirit is rejuvenated. You can now see, hear, and focus; your chain of emotional bondage is broken, and you can thank God, as noted in Col 3:10 (NIV).

The Spiritual Ingredient Mix for Accessorizing Your Temple

4. Long-suffering comes from the Greek word "*makrothumia*," meaning "makes" for "long," and "*thumos*" for "temper" is usually rendered "long suffering."[2] A long-suffering individual shows great restraint under duress when stirred to anger. This reference is to an individual who is not provoked into seeking retaliation against another whom they believe has wronged them. This seems prevalent in today's twenty-first century, with a tendency to seek retaliation against anyone who does not support their ideology, whether right or wrong, within or outside the rule of law. It is similar to going back and forth, seeking anyone who stands in their way. This seems so similar to Satan, seeking to inflict pain, cause destruction, and sever believers' faith and trust in God. Have you ever held dangerous feelings toward another person? Be careful; such pinned-up emotional turmoil may cause you to lose your Christlike character.

In Exod 34:6, God is the source of long-suffering because it is part of his character. Long-suffering is putting up with others who treat you wrongfully, yet you must love them unconditionally. This isn't easy! And if the believer is not careful, this accessory may cause them to falter. Long-suffering is described as having a Christlike character, equipping you as a believer to grow in God's grace and providing the spiritual discipline needed to sustain blatant hardship. Long-suffering means putting up with adult children when you have done all you possibly can, and there remains an attitude of entitlement. You love your child, but at what point do you cut the umbilical cord? As a believer, you will endure the hardship of people putting you down, setting traps, holding back information, sometimes being untruthful and jealous, and sometimes laying obstacles in your path to delay or sidetrack you. First Corinthians 13:4 tells you, "Love suffers long and is kind; love does not envy; love does not parade itself, is not puffed up." Therefore, long-suffering is a form of patience in the face of endurance. When you become upset or distraught

2. Davey, "What Is the Meaning."

Accessorization

over the things people do to you, imagine how Jesus must have felt when he endured all the pain and suffering for your past, present, and future transgressions. So, before you think about or commit a transgression, remember that Jesus has already paid the price. He is the perfect model, and God has the final judgment.

5. Gentleness ("*prautes*," Greek for "gentleness," "meekness of humility," "mildness of manners or disposition")[3] is the fifth and most powerful characteristic of the fruit of the Spirit, reflecting God's character. It is a strength under duress, rooted in God's love. It is a way of life that is pleasing to God. As a member of the body of Christ, this characteristic requires you to be kind, caring, humble, compassionate, and tenderhearted to others. Sometimes, believers in the body of Christ may, like the world, admire the friendly, soft-spoken, and caring individual as a meek person, not necessarily weak. There are several key aspects of gentleness in the Bible. These terms or key accessories are familiar to believers and have been experienced or utilized in their daily walk with the Lord.

These accessories are not always easy to implement, but are necessary for followers of Christ. They are:[4]

   a. **Humility and Meekness.** People often assume that these two concepts are signs of weakness. These accessories demonstrate strong character because the individual is willing to submit themselves to God's will, not self-will, and is not overly impressed by their own importance. You have met the type and may have been conversing with them. Remember the "I did it" person. Perhaps they seldom give God credit for anything. As you reflect, have you ever found yourself in this situation, or do you authentically give all praise to the Lord? Jesus tells us in Matt 5, the Beatitudes, verse 5, "Blessed are the meek,

---

3. *Merriam-Webster*, "Gentleness."
4. Institute in Basic Life Principles, "Gentleness vs. Harshness."

for they will inherit the earth." Notice that Jesus did not say "may inherit" or "might inherit"; Jesus clearly stated they "will inherit the earth." Have you considered your achievements self-accomplished, or thought yourself self-absorbed or self-directed? Where are you?

b. **Compassion and Kindness.** These individuals have a sensitive heart for others and support them in their struggles. They may volunteer their time at the food pantry or homeless shelter, serving meals during the week or on holidays, especially Thanksgiving. Some golfers participate in tournaments and raise funds for scholarships or other humanitarian causes. This particular key may bring to remembrance Stephen and the women in need as found in the book of Acts 6 and 7. This situation is prevalent in some parts of today's society, where complaints arise that people of a particular social group are being overlooked, not because of who they are (God's children), but rather because of how they are perceived (based on ethnicity, culture, and class). Compassion is of the heart.

c. **Patience and Forbearance** (God's holding back judgment or punishment and extending grace and mercy). Where would the world be if God decided today was the day to unleash his judgment on humanity, but instead, each day your eyes open to a new day filled with God's grace and his abundant mercy? Remember Jesus, who was punished at Calvary, held no aught against man, and he still intercedes on your behalf. Gentleness is key, especially when dealing with different situations or people. Thank God for his grace, mercy, and patience in the face of our daily sins and transgressions, which are created daily.

As believers, you must be patient and understanding of your fellow believers. It is not easy, but if you have given your life to Christ and believe in and study his word, you know what is expected of you as a believer. It is not easy to have patience, but you were taught to have it

Accessorization

because someone will have patience for you one day. An excellent example of forbearance is the scenario between David and Saul; David could have taken Saul's life, but he did not.

    d. **Restoration and Not Judgment.** Ah! Difficult, you might say. But look at the costs Jesus paid to restore you to oneness, *koinonia* (fellowship), and a personal relationship with God. This segment is described as a gentle approach to correcting or rebuking others, with a focus on restoring rather than judging. Some of you believers love and firmly judge, and I know it is not easy. Judging seems to come easily. Is it judging, or am I stating an opinion? You decide and remember only God judges. It is only by God's grace.

    Think about restoring a piece of furniture. You must first remove the old covering, paint, or stain, then sand to smooth rough edges and uneven surfaces. That is what Jesus did for you: he smoothed you out, sanded you over, dipped you in the blood of the Lamb to wash you over and make you clean. You now enjoy the newness of life, like the piece of old furniture made to look new again. You don't see any blemishes, but the old wood stands out as new.

6. Goodness "signifies those moral qualities described by the adjective *agathos*." Goodness is a reflection of God's benevolent nature.[5] I often associate goodness and kindness with grace and mercy. Goodness reflects God's nature and the characteristics of his followers. It is the presence of both your outer and inner accessories, righteousness, and living a pleasing and acceptable lifestyle to God. As the senior saints would say, "You can't straddle the fence," meaning you can't have one foot in the church and one in the world. This initiates a struggle between the flesh and the Spirit; you must decide which you will serve and give your allegiance to. God's goodness is seen in justice, wisdom, and grace. You can't earn, create, develop,

---

5. Vine et al., *Vine's Expository Dictionary*, 165.

copy, clone, or reproduce goodness because God gives it to you through his Holy Spirit (Gal 6:10). Goodness involves believers seeking virtue and living in accordance with ethical principles designed by God, and reflecting his nature or his will. A believer who demonstrates goodness in their life aims to promote change in different settings. A believer who adheres to the characteristics of goodness is a person who believes in righteousness, morality, generosity, integrity, and virtue. The goodness of God characterizes his moral nature, benevolence, compassion, unconditional love, faithfulness, and gracious mercy.

7. Faith ("*pistis*" is Greek for "faith"; also means "belief" or "trust") Faith "signifies both the character of God and the responsibility and expectation of you as a believer."[6] You have all been taught that you must have faith like a mustard seed, which is very tiny, but when it is produced, the plant is large and full. This tells you that with small faith, you can be bountifully blessed, with enough that the overflow can be poured on others. I believe in that faith and have experienced God's bountiful favor. In Rom 5:2, it is written, "Because of our faith, Christ has brought us into this place of undeserved privilege where you now stand, and you confidently and joyfully look forward to sharing God's glory." Be faithful in your walk as a believer, and do not allow the snares set up for you as believers to deter you from the word of God. Please don't succumb to flattery; it is temporal and will lead nowhere. Be mindful of the little things, as noted in Luke 16:10 (NIV): "Whoever can be trusted with very little can also be trusted with much, and whoever is dishonest with very little will also be dishonest with much." Faith encompasses loyalty, truth, and adherence to God's promises and duties. God's unchanging nature is that he is the Keeper of promises; he is the Alpha and the Omega, the beginning and the end. How authentic is your faith?

---

6. *Merriam-Webster*, "Faith."

Accessorization

8. Meekness. The word used for meekness in Greek is *prautes*, which connotes a total lack of self-concern. "Meekness is essentially an attitude or quality of the heart whereby a person is willing to accept and submit without resistance to the will and desire of someone else."[7] Therefore, Matt 5:5 states, "Blessed are the meek, for they shall inherit the earth." God expects humility from his children, and for you to grow and develop in your efforts to accessorize your Christian character. These spiritual nuggets are like some of the great characters adorned with Jesus, who is the greatest role model of himself. Sterk and Scazzero in *Christian Character* wrote "that some people can't take their eyes off themselves and their inadequacies, while others swing like a pendulum from one extreme to the other."[8] Some people see themselves as highly accomplished and productive, as though they got on the rock amid the pond alone. No one can tell them anything; they made it, they got it, and now they don't owe the world a thing—and sometimes have difficulty sharing. They sit on their rock like turtles, admiring the world from their vantage point. They would understand who had brought them this far if they stopped to think and reflect on their path. Be truthful as a believer, remain trustworthy, and, above all challenges, keep your integrity. Don't sell yourself short for a title, perceived power, or control; human greed will ultimately come to an end, then what? One of God's divine commands is that God hates a liar, as stated in Prov 12:22: "The Lord detests lying lips, but he delights in trustworthy people." Are you trustworthy? Do you give God credit for your success? Your accomplishments?

9. Temperance (*"enkrateia"* and *"sophrosyne"* in Greek is "self-control" or "self-constraint") is the quality of moderation or emotional self-restraint or control over actions, thoughts, and feelings: "The whole multitude of men lack temperance

---

7. Caner, "Spiritual Meekness."
8. Sterk and Scazzero, *Christian Character*, 4.

The Spiritual Ingredient Mix for Accessorizing Your Temple

in their lives, either from ignorance or want of self-control."[9] It is a righteous habit that enables a person to govern their natural appetite for the pleasures of the senses by the norms prescribed by reason and to show restraint. It is crucial to have self-control in your daily life, irrespective of the intensity of the issue. Have self-control, as noted in 1 Cor 9:25: "He controls his body and puts it under his discipline so that others will not be tempted to imitate him." If you have control over your temperament, this indicates that you have been transformed, as Paul states, by renewing your mind. Those former things you did when you had no experience of Christ and the Holy Spirit in your life are dead and no longer control your spirit. The most outstanding example and role model of temperance is when Jesus cleansed the temple; he showed righteous anger without losing his temper (Matt 9:10–17). Maintaining self-control is most difficult for me when unexpected adversarial circumstances arise on a Zoom call that I am leading. There may be a challenger who continues to be disruptive; this is a deep pool that only the power of God can intercede in: and through the Holy Spirit; a pathway is created that does not hurt or embarrass anyone (Titus 1:8). Be holy because God is holy (1 Pet 1:16). Your actions and words set you apart, and you dedicate your life to God. Your life should be a model for "moral purity." God expects you to live and do as he commands/instructs. He expects you, as a believer, to strive to reflect on him in everything you do and say. Your character should mature daily as you walk with God, using the spiritual gift(s) God has given you as a believer through the Holy Spirit to edify the body of Christ, to help one another grow in grace, and become spiritually mature in knowledge and understanding.

---

9. Plato, *Laws* 5.

2. Building Spiritual Muscles—Accessories for Developing Spiritual Growth

Anyone who listens to your teaching and follows it is wise, like a person who builds a house on solid rock. Though the rain comes in torrents and the floodwaters rise and the winds beat against that house, it won't collapse because it is built on bedrock.

Matt 7:24-25 NLT

"The three types of muscle tissue are cardiac, smooth, and skeletal (striated). Cardiac muscle is found only in the heart, while smooth muscle is found in the digestive system, blood vessels, bladder, airways, and uterus. Skeletal muscle is the type of muscle that you can see and feel."[10] These muscles play a critical role in vital functions of the human body.

The spiritual body is equally important to the human body and plays an authentic role in its daily functioning. If the human body is plagued by stressors affecting the pancreas, heart, lungs, kidneys, and critical muscular functions, it is not in harmony. Each body part is connected to and affects the others. Scripture tells you that there are many parts but one body. If societal and personal issues block the body's critical functioning, then it does not function at a level in which God can use you in kingdom-building. God expects you to eliminate old hurts you may have harbored for years. These old hurts are like stagnant, unchanging, lingering swamp water. Because they are neither moving nor running, they give birth to green algae, and nothing of substance can survive. These are the issues of pain and mistreatment you have allowed others to "dump" upon you, causing you to suffer, perhaps quietly in your inner self or openly. Life has moved you to better circumstances and new challenges, yet you remain stagnant—like stagnant swamp water—stale and unable to move because of negative emotions. God expects you to move forward, let go, and let him deal with your hurt and pain so that you can forgive the initiator

---

10. Freudenrich, "How Muscles Work."

The Spiritual Ingredient Mix for Accessorizing Your Temple

of your circumstance, so that you can learn to forgive yourself. This forgiveness is a two-pronged process necessary to help you begin developing spiritual muscles, serving as a crack in the door that supports spiritual growth and maturity. How do you test your spiritual growth? Mulholland tells you to examine the nature and quality of your relationships with others. He continues: "Are you more loving, compassionate, patient, understanding, caring, giving, and forgiving than you were a year ago?"[11] I challenge you to take a reflective test. Suppose your answer is not authentic, and others in your circle cannot express your behavior in a positive light. In that case, your spiritual growth becomes stagnant, and you are still in the swamp of life. You are caught up in yesterday's pain and anguish; you may not even recall how you took the wrong path. The swamp's deceptive appearance covers its true depth and inherent dangers, where you can be easily misguided and inextricably trapped. Your negative behavior indicates that you need to take action; otherwise, you will continue to be negative, unforgiving, and bitter, striking out at others with the venom of the rattler you encountered in the swamp. If you cannot express God's love or understand all that he has done for you with the sacrifice of his Son, then you, as Mulholland expresses, need to examine the nature of your spiritual life and growth carefully. I have been on the short end of a sister's rope and have felt and experienced her anguish with full hurricane fury. It is so excruciating, and it made me wonder: where is God in her life? Is this a judgmental call? Perhaps! I find myself asking God to forgive me if I said anything to hurt my Christian sister. I don't want to be a stumbling block in anyone's spiritual growth and development. Her behavior has made me, a believer, a teacher of his word, and a follower of his instructions, to question myself and critically examine how my words may have been perceived. I know what God expects of me as a believer, and when I find myself in the grip of the alligator's jaws, caught off guard, in those crucial moments, my only thought is survival. And I, too, need some reflection.

---

11. Mulholland. *Invitation*, 50.

Accessorization

Imagine the pain Jesus must have experienced. He was innocent of all charges and did not deserve the cruelty and anguish bestowed upon him. Think about and reflect on your imagination: a crown of thorns being pressed into your head until the blood begins to run down; yet he asked his father to forgive them because they did not know what they were doing. You may consider this to be the first doctrine of forgiveness. This declaration was made after he suffered humiliation, false accusations, and painful and dreadful punishment. He was forced to carry his weighted wooden cross to Calvary so that he would suffer the agony of crucifixion. They added punishment to degradation. They wanted to ensure his death, so they drove spikes into his feet and nails into his hands, pierced him in his side, and gave him vinegar to quench his thirst. What if Jesus had decided that this pain was too great to suffer and die for people who displayed so many dysfunctional attitudes? What if God held a grudge against the Romans who killed his Son in such a painful way? What if God had not forgiven their transgressions, or Jesus had said, "Father, I don't want to endure this pain?" Where would we be? Where would we be? But Jesus endured the suffering and agony. So, as a believer, you reflect on Jesus's agony at Calvary and look at all he suffered from the day he entered the city, knowing full well the fate he would suffer. Remember that through all the agony, Christ's body was bruised but never broken. So, through spiritual accessorization, you must learn to cope with stressors that may impact your spiritual growth. Learning to pray and ask God for guidance in handling disruptions in your daily life has impacted your inner being and relationships. God empowers you daily, giving you the strength to meet the challenges that continuously plague your environment: challenges of violence, inequality in programs and services, and discrimination that have been with you since biblical times. And simply dealing with people in general.

Believers seek spiritual things to improve their skills, abilities, inner selves, relationships, and fellowship with God and one another. Those accessories that give you confidence cover your physical and emotional flaws and environmental trauma that impact safety

The Spiritual Ingredient Mix for Accessorizing Your Temple

and a sense of self. Spiritual accessorization has certain privileges for the believer, which allow you to know who you are and the benefits of being in God's database. Do you meet the eligibility criteria for membership in his database? How can you become a carrier of spiritual accessorization? The application process contains the accessories of belief, confession, repentance, acceptance, baptism, and following God's plan for you as a believer (Eph 3).

The work ahead for believers in making new disciples for Christ is even more critical. There is constant destruction and upheaval. We are like spiritual contractors, moving along to restore, reclaim, and redirect those who have lost their way, those who never found it, and those who fear becoming disconnected along the way. We must instill the word of the gospel of good news. It is not new; it is just presented differently to show the way. We must, as change agents for God, stand firm on his word, be intentional in our work, stand for right and truth, and be bold enough to stare the enemy in the eyes.

It is essential to build a strong biblical foundation. There are many gods, but we are building on the only true God, who has divine and holy power to protect those who believe in him. He has all the essential tools for the battleground. The adversary has many followers who adhere to his words and teachings, but they will not endure his teachings. God of all is indispensable. He is the Alpha and the Omega; the beginning and the end. We must continue to be prayerful and maintain our focus, discerning the rhetoric and recognizing its sound, so that we are not caught off guard. As we face life's challenges, things may become overwhelming, but remember that we serve an all-powerful, mighty God who remains in control.

Be mindful of the things God has done for you. He blessed you when you did not deserve it, forgave you when he could have extinguished your life, and gives you unmerited grace and favor each morning. Please remember that he is everywhere at once; he knows your every thought and each strand of hair on your head. Ps 8:4 (NIV) states, "What is man that you are mindful of him, the son of man, that you care for him?"

3. Accessories for Developing a Positive Self-Image from Carnality to Spirituality

The mind of a sinful man is death, but the mind controlled by the Spirit is life and peace; the sinful mind is hostile to God. It does not submit to God's law, nor can it do so. Those controlled by the sinful nature cannot please God.

Rom 8:6–8

The following areas can help you accessorize your attitude and cultivate greater self-awareness. In addition, it helps enhance your unique personal lifestyle by connecting elements that build a positive self-image and transition you from carnality to spirituality. Consider the connection between the Vine and the branches, which ensures a selfless life stream and a consistent desire to search for truth, thereby developing an authentic ability to care about others. Learn self-restraint as you, a believer, continue to grow and develop from the nourishment of the Vine. Through your connection to the Vine, you can better discern the difference between carnality and spirituality, as well as inauthentic behaviors in society. You do not become prey to their offerings. A carnal mind is full of the desires and pleasures of the world. A carnal-minded person will do anything their heart desires to feel good and satisfied, such as disregarding the rule of law and uniquely manipulating the minds and emotions of others so that they believe this is the correct and only way. A carnal-minded person, and you probably see them every day, focuses on those things that are earthly, fleshly, and desirous. This type of individual prioritizes the satisfaction of bodily appetites and impulses, which reminds you of the craving of the Epicurean, who found happiness through simple pleasures, which is the ultimate goal. As you study God's word, you will understand that these persons are disobedient to his word, are constantly struggling with inner turmoil, seeking material possessions, and are self-centered. On the other hand, a spiritually minded person is genuinely concerned about others. They are consistent, selfless, search for truth, and do not seek or run after worldly and fleshly pleasures for satisfaction. The spiritually minded person is focused on God, seeking to learn about spiritual matters and things that are of a spiritual nature. They seek to learn more about God, striving to live by his will, following God's commands, instructions, and his precepts. These are the believers who are knowledgeable about the fruit of the Spirit, its characteristics, and its importance in their daily lives. They are like King Solomon; riches were not of great interest to him. He had a kingdom to manage and wanted to be fair in all his decisions. He asked God for wisdom, and with wisdom comes knowledge, understanding, and discernment. If you had the opportunity to ask, "What do you want?" could you do what Solomon did?

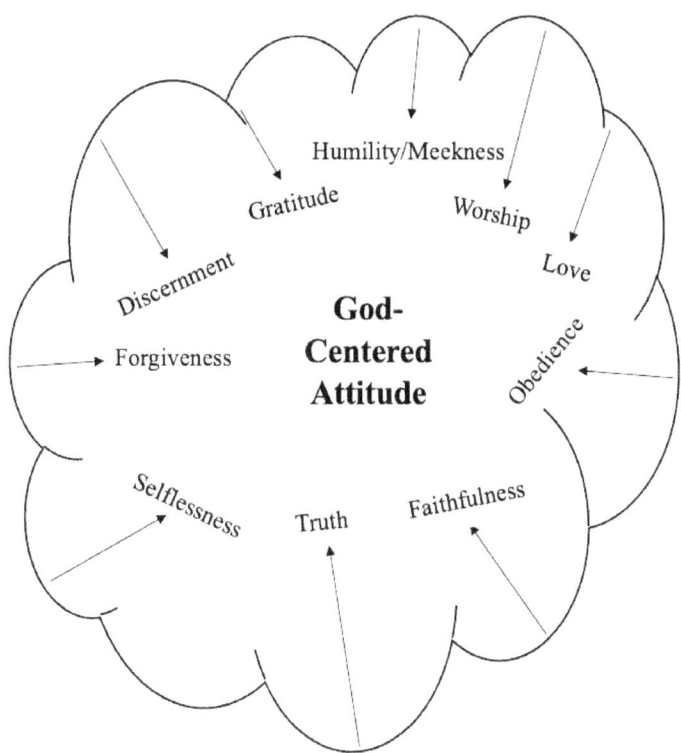

Characteristics For A God-Centered Attitude
Developed by Doris Bourgeois Turner 5/2025

Accessorization

Building positive self-esteem, self-image, and confidence begins in childhood. In Jean Illsley Clark's book *Self-Esteem: A Family Affair*, "the home and family are the first places you decide, observe, and practice how to be that way."[12] The family circle is where you feel or experience love, warmth, and forgiveness; these elements are just a few that help build positive self-esteem and nurture. The give-and-take in a family structure builds good character. In contrast, a home filled with negative emotions and a household in bitter turmoil breeds a child who may feel unloved, insecure, bitter, isolated, and angry. The list is endless; they may erupt like a volcano spewing molten rocks, ash, and fire, or their emotions may be like a dark cloud filled with wind, rain, and hail, forming a massive tornado that rips apart anything in its path. A child must be taught the values and morals that are intrinsic to his growth and development, as well as his success or failure in society. A child does not live in a safe and loving environment where they can develop a sense of relationship and hear and receive words and actions that say "I love you," which may lead to a life of confusion, inability to make choices and decisions, does not know how to relate to other people, and may harbor feelings of neglect that may lead to public statistics. This child must learn to make choices and live by the consequences of those choices. The child must also learn to develop relationships, but these skills are often underdeveloped because they did not experience them in their early family life. Does the child have a sense of family?

God instructs you in 2 Cor 5:21 to be righteous because he is righteous. You can only be righteous through faith in our Lord and Savior, Jesus Christ. God made him who is sinless to be sin for you so that in Jesus you might become the righteousness of God. Be fruitful, multiply, be productive, replenish the earth, and control the garden and everything within it. God expected this of Adam and Eve when he created them in the garden of Eden. Genesis 1:28 (NIV) states, "God blessed them and said, 'Be fruitful and increase in number; fill the earth and subdue it." But someplace in time, they lent their ear to the sweet whispers of the serpent, became

---

12. Clarke, *Self-Esteem*, 4.

The Spiritual Ingredient Mix for Accessorizing Your Temple

disobedient against the word of God, sinned, and were expelled from Eden. You are learning the doctrine of forgiveness (for yourself and others) so that your temple remains clean and is not filled with clutter so you can't find your way out. There is so much clutter that it is difficult to distinguish between genuine content and junk. Too many choices lead to indecisiveness, irrationality, and confusion. God forgave our sins that began with disobedience in the garden of Eden with Adam and Eve through the blood, death, and resurrection of Jesus Christ.

A believer's life is so bombarded by so many choices that God's word must reside within so that they will not succumb to negative influences that may penetrate their thinking. God's word should become a part of their internal operating system. Some of these choices concern the right direction a believer must take when seeking help to find his way, just as the prodigal son did. Other decisions in life may leave you feeling downtrodden, perplexed, and overwhelmed by life's challenges while seeking the right leader to help you make the right choice that will guide you in restoring your faith when you come to a crossroads in life. The leader must know and understand the word of God so that they can assure you. His word will help you make correct choices through spiritual discernment, enabling you to be righteous and know that God loves you.

There is restoration in:

A. Quiet

"Teach me, and I will be quiet." It isn't easy to relate to or work with people who talk without listening to others. Have you ever observed two people in a conversation? You would think that one person is listening while the other is talking, but in most situations, both are speaking simultaneously and not hearing each other. A conversation should be a participatory exchange of ideas, thoughts, feelings, and emotions among people engaged in the process. Observing the conversation as it progresses is both exciting and stressful; the longer the interaction, the louder their voices become as each person competes to express their opinion. If they are not careful, agitation enters the conversation, and discretion is no longer an obstacle. Gentleness, kindness, and respect become intertwined as frustration builds. Now, each has allowed themselves to become a part of a public display. How can you encourage the receiver and the sender of words, thoughts, ideas, emotions, and feelings to listen deeply to what the other person is communicating? Communication through conversation is essential for developing relationships, character, and spiritual growth. It teaches the ability to listen, which is sometimes overlooked when each person is trying to get their point across. God is trying to get your attention, but you have become too busy with nonessential activities, events, and conversations, and you can't hear him because he is whispering to you. You must tune in to your surroundings to engage in conversation. Through the working of the Holy Spirit, you can ask God to teach you when and how to listen and be quiet to hear the results of your conversation. As you reflect on various conversations with someone, do you see yourself as an active listener during those conversations? Are you an active sender or listener? Do you hear? Are you in tune with your surroundings? Take a moment to listen quietly in the early morning and pay attention to what you hear. What have you missed?

B. Correction

"Show me where I need to be corrected." This illustrates where and how you need to correct a mistake, how you set a wrong right, and how you correct or remove a fault that is not pleasing to others or, more importantly, to God. According to *Merriam-Webster*, "corrected" means "to make true, accurate, or right: remove the errors or faults from."[13] In Prov 12:1, the Bible speaks about "corrected" or "correct," which says, "Whoever loves discipline, loves knowledge, and who hates reproof is stupid." There may have been times when someone has corrected you on your journey,

---

13. *Merriam-Webster*, "Correction."

but the correction is not the issue. How you are corrected is what becomes memorable. If someone properly corrects you with love and compassion, you welcome it because you know that, as you are corrected for the mistakes and errors you make, it indicates your desire for knowledge and spiritual growth. Correction should not be an issue if it is done lovingly, kindly, and compassionately to help you grow in grace. Correction raises its ugly head when done to embarrass, overpower, or insult the intelligence and integrity of the other person. You can be corrected. However, some attempts to fix it may allow the old self to be injected into what could be a moment of training.

Chastisement and instructions are words found in Scripture and can be administered by the Holy Spirit. The Holy Spirit can rebuke you, and all of this is done to enhance your spiritual growth and development, giving you a sense of direction when conversations, issues, or situations go offtrack. Have you ever been corrected? As you reflect, what was your experience like?

C. Words

How painful are honest words? Exceptionally painful yet rewarding, if told in a loving, compassionate, and teaching manner, words cut profoundly and force you to bleed the truth. Words can make or break you, guide or cause you to lose your direction, cloud or clear the path, and confuse or direct you to a better way of life. Words can lift you to a higher level by teaching you about God and his holy words, love, expectations, favor, miracles, passion, and the sacrifice of his only Son, who gave his life for you. Words can be deceptive, causing you to fall out of favor with God. Through propaganda, they can lead those who hear the same phrasing to eventually believe an untruth or half-truth as the whole truth, similar to what Satan did with Eve in Eden. A few words can be taken out of context and presented as correct, or used in context with slight variations. You must have spiritual discernment and ask God to keep your ears attuned to his sacred words so that through wisdom, you can discern a deceptive will and unrighteous motives.

Accessorization

Words can be as painful as surgery without anesthesia. Our brain stores painful memories and experiences, serving as a stimulus to avoid situations that may cause pain. As children, many of you may have played a game called "sticks and stones," which included the phrase "Sticks and stones may break my bones, but words don't bother me." You may recall this game vividly because the sticks or stones hit the body and initiated pain; the thinking was that words do not hit the flesh; therefore, there is no pain. As you grow and mature, children's play games can become cruel, and you learn that words hurt; they hurt you emotionally, psychologically, and physically, and sometimes, a simple apology does not remove the sting of the word(s). The apology simply makes the perpetrator feel better, not the victim. Based on Prov 18:21, words can encourage or destroy you. I am reminded of my eldest granddaughter when she was about two years old. She would come to visit us with her mom, and her favorite spot was the brick landing in front of the fireplace; it was her stage. She would pretend to sing, dance, or give a speech with such confidence and enthusiasm. Although we could not understand the words of a two-year-old, we would clap for her and encourage her. She has worked in theater; possesses confidence, self-esteem, and self-assurance; and speaks very well. We could have discouraged her, and she might have become too dependent. We accessorized her skills and abilities with positive feedback. Treat the words of a despairing man as wind. The wind comes and goes. In Eph 4:29, the Bible addresses communication, stating: "Let no corrupting talk come out of your mouths, but only such as is suitable for building up, as fits the occasion, that it may give grace to those who hear." Please continue to encourage with positive words and positive body language that promotes confidence and assurance, letting children know you care about them.

D. Arguments

What do they prove? Arguments prove absolutely nothing; there are no spiritual benefits in arguing. Physical detriment is emotionally harmful to the body, causing headaches, increased blood pressure, a rapid heart rate, and increased pounding on the heart, along with other emotional stressors. In Prov 20:3, you are expected to "avoid a fight which is a mark of honor; only fools insist on arguing." People who are friends and may also be related have gotten into a heated, severe argument over a game of checkers: do you take a long jump or play over the board; can the king jump anyway? It continues until one person becomes frustrated and walks away from the game. Sometimes, a more mature, spiritually inclined bystander will bring some sense to the senseless arguing and, with words of wisdom, reunite the group. These similar senseless scenarios have been the impetus for quarrels, gang violence, shootings, and other acts of violence. Scriptures instruct believers not to quarrel but to find alternative ways to manage anger, resentment, and frustration. Arguing proves nothing and derives from "a lack of mutual, empathic understanding." The Bible encourages you to avoid foolish, unproductive arguments that do not add to or complement the edification of the body of Christ. As believers, you must focus on the nine spiritual characteristics in Gal 5.

Just as you have accessories to make your physical body look attractive and feel good about yourself, you should also have spiritual accessories that enhance your spiritual self and help you see the presence of the Holy Spirit without verbalizing that he lives within you. God has given you, as believers, unique characteristics that should be a part of your daily lifestyle. These are the fruit of the Spirit, and each day, as you put on your physical makeup and check yourselves in the mirror to ensure you are together, your spiritual selves must be suited to guard you for the battle. God made you in his image, and through that image, you have the indwelling of the Holy Spirit, who guides, directs, convicts, corrects, and leads you to follow the expectations he laid out for you in Gal 5:21–22 and the commandments in Exodus.

Each day, you face new challenges, expectations, and obstacles. But take heart, for God has given you his word as a guiding light. It offers instructions to help you navigate these hurdles. Every morning, as you wake up to the enormity of his goodness and blessings, you can find solace in the fact that you are not alone

Accessorization

in your struggles. However, with each new day, there will be hills to climb, valleys to explore, and mountains to conquer. You must ask God to help you cleanse your hearts and minds of anger, which can block his mercies.

Remember, you are not alone in your daily battles.

1) **Stay Smart for Safety.** Keep congruent things together. You must also avoid sharing too many concerns with people and friends; they may be like frayed electric cords that constantly emit currents, causing confusion and potentially leading to total disruption. Don't overload.

2) **Stay Focused.** Let your eyes open, looking out for spiritual leaks, like the mascara that runs down your face when touched by tears or sweat. If it is run less freely, everything is held together like a volcano waiting to erupt. You must be cautious when associating with unsaved individuals; if you do, ensure you are not caught off guard. Watch for leaks, such as falling into the group norm and saying or doing things that are out of character for your spiritual self. People have a unique way of making you think it is OK; follow your discerned spirit. Stay focused, and don't let these leaks distract you from your spiritual journey. Remember, your commitment to this journey will keep you on the right path.

3) **Upgrade Your Spiritual System.** Keep up your inner self-accessorization just as you do with your outer self-appearance. In 1 Pet 3:3–4, you are instructed not to be concerned about the outward beauty of fancy hairstyles, colorful nails, expensive jewelry, or beautiful clothes. Instead, you should be more concerned with the beauty from within—the unfading beauty of a gentle and quiet spirit, which is very precious to God. Holy women of old, according to 1 Peter, made themselves beautiful from within, nurturing their inner spirit. These women placed their trust in God and accepted their husbands' authority. This was a similar factor in the 2024 election; some men wanted women to obey their husbands, just as their foremothers had. You must ensure that all accessories

The Spiritual Ingredient Mix for Accessorizing Your Temple

blend well and complement each other. What is your spiritual system? Does your heart, spirit, soul, and mind work harmoniously to keep you aligned with God's word and his expectations of you as a believer? God has assured you that all things work together for your good if you have a relationship with him. You will have suffering, but as you conform to Christ's image, you will grow in spiritual maturity (Rom 8:28).

4. Public Image—Who's Watching?

Be wise in how you act toward outsiders; make the most of every opportunity. Let your conversation be always full of grace, seasoned with salt, so that you may know how to answer everyone.
COL 4:5–6

Your public image is the initial perception people have of you as an individual, encompassing how you present yourself and whether it is perceived as positive or negative. This perception can impact your personal and professional lifestyle for the remainder of your life. This image encompasses personal traits, including how you manage yourself under stress, your values and morals, and your Christian lifestyle. This public image becomes a crucial factor if you aspire to run for public office. If the image is positive and your opponent has the impression that you are winning, there is a probability that they may seek negativity to divert you offtrack and sow doubt in the minds of your supporters. Every rock and fold in your life is unturned; it can become ruthless. You may want to consider being mindful of your virtual communication.

The *Longman Dictionary of Contemporary English* defines public image as the "character or attitudes that most people think they have and try to improve."[14] A good public image is one that encompasses the fruit of the Spirit and the image of Christ, as described in the book of Genesis. The characteristics of this image

---

14. Longman, "Public Image."

Accessorization

become crucial when seeking a political career. If the image has been positive, it may be full speed ahead, or is it? Sometimes, very innocent things posted on Facebook, Instagram, and YouTube years earlier can come to deter your life's dream. The virtual world, while it may seem simplistic and perfectly innocent, controls your life and brings everything to a standstill. Even if you are innocent and there is no "dirt," someone can fabricate and, with AI, make it appear truthful. Your personal and private image is you; guard it, and try to live a life that pleases God.

You must live wisely in your relationships with those who are nonbelievers, but, at the same time, be wise as a serpent, as some believers may not be who you think they are. There may be some people who look to you, given your lifestyle, as a positive role model to help them on their spiritual journey. You must be mindful of your actions and careful with your words and tone when interacting with others. God is watching you! He is everywhere at once. He hears and knows your thoughts before the words are formed and spew out from your mouth. He knows what you will say before the words form in your thoughts and flow from your mouth. God is everywhere, omnipresent. He is everywhere at once. He hears what you say and knows what you will do before you do it. He knows what you think before you speak it. This section of the book presents several thought-provoking questions for believers to consider. It elicits different thoughts and reflections based on individual experiences, spiritual maturity, and cultural background.

Where is your hope? Your hope is in the grace of God. You must repent for the sins that may hold you in bondage, such as jealousy, envy, deceit, gossiping about each other, and being disrespectful. You must seek God, ask him to restore you, and let him be the center of your life. Let God live within you. You believe that what God has done for another, he will do the same for you. You must trust and believe in God and what he has in store for you. He will reward you at his discretion. As you move through the accessorization process, do you ever allow your friends or a particular situation to control or influence you? If so, how does this impact your personal and spiritual image? No problem or friend should ever control your life if you are free and believe in the Lord and Savior, Jesus Christ. If you love and trust God, different experiences, painful situations, and circumstances will be worked out through faith in him. Don't be afraid to say no to friends, especially when you know the problem is incorrect and will not please God. If your friends are participating in an activity or act that makes you feel uncomfortable, it is OK to excuse yourself or discreetly leave.

Who is watching? The most crucial person who controls everything and knows all. Proverbs 15:3 tells us that the Lord is watching everything, keeping a close eye on both the good and the evil, as well as the just and the unjust. We must continue to spread the gospel of good news, and by doing this, we are serving God.

5. Keeping Your Temple Pure—Accessorized Under New Management

Therefore, I urge you, brothers, in view of God's mercy, to offer your bodies as living sacrifices, holy and pleasing to God—this is your spiritual act of worship.

ROM 12:1 NIV

When we hear the word "temple," we are referring to a holy place, a building or structure similar to the church or synagogue, where believers give God corporate worship, praise, and thanksgiving. The physical body, that temple in which the Holy Spirit, given to believers in the book of Acts, took residence, when Jesus ascended to the Father, and did not want to leave us comfortless. The Holy Spirit's role is to give direction, provide clarification, instructions, and guidance, and, at the same time, instill correction, discipline, and reproof. "In the hermeneutical studies of the premodern church, for example, the temple is (1) the mystical 'body' of all God's faithful people (the temple's 'allegorical' sense), (2) the faithful soul of each genuine believer (the temple's 'tropological' sense),

Accessorization

and (3) the centre of God's eschatological reign on Earth (the 'anagogical sense)."[15]

You are not speaking about the place where God's people go to be in his presence to praise and worship him; you are, however, talking about the physical self, and your body is the dwelling place for the Holy Spirit given to you in the book of Acts when Jesus ascended to the Father and did not want to leave you comfortless. The building or structure is a holy place similar to your church, where you give God cooperative worship, praise, and thanksgiving. The physical body is that temple in which the Holy Spirit takes residence in the body of the believer to give directions, provide clarification, instructions, and guidance, and at the same time, instill correction, discipline, and reproof.

In 2 Cor 6:19–20, God tells you that your body is the temple of the Holy Spirit, where he lives in you, and your body is not your own. Because the Holy Spirit lives within you, God expects you to keep your body sacred like the holy temple (structure); it is a place of worship, a sacred dominion, a place that should not be defiled by drugs or alcohol, illicit sexual immorality, but these temples should be held in reverence because of who dwells there. Because your body is the residence of the Holy Spirit, you are now under new management, under the rule and plan of God for your life. As believers, you must understand the enormity and importance of the resident who dwells within you. Imagine having the supernatural power of God within you, who goes where you go, hears what you say, and knows what you will do before you do. You must ensure that you eat properly; treat your body like a physical building, accessorizing it with nourishing and healthy food. By practicing healthy eating habits, you may help prevent illnesses such as high blood pressure, diabetes, lung and kidney disease, and other ailments that can harm your body. These diseases limit your availability to God. As believers living in a borrowed temple, you need to exercise more to ensure that the temple is built on a solid foundation, unlike two of the three little pigs, whose houses, when the wind blew and the rain poured, were swallowed up by the storm.

15. Cook, "Temple in the Christian Bible."

The Spiritual Ingredient Mix for Accessorizing Your Temple

In medicine, "the temple, also known as the pterion, is located on the side of the head behind the eye between the forehead and the ear is the side of the head behind the eyes." However, the Holy Bible tells you that your temple is sacred, and where the Holy Spirit abides, you must keep it clean. God clearly tells you in 1 Cor 6:17 that if anyone destroys his temple, he will destroy them. You must get enough rest to keep your temple and related parts alert. Learn to manage your stressors, which are high killers of your body, leading to strokes, heart attacks, migraine headaches, swelling in the ankles, arthritis in the knees, hips, and back, and swollen legs, forcing you to ingest drugs and chemicals to sustain your temple. If you are not careful, chemicals and drugs can lead to more significant pain and deprivation. You are not in control of your body; it is a gift from God for God's purpose, and you must, therefore, keep it running in undamaged shape so that God can use you for the sake of others. While you are living in this temporary shelter, please ensure that there are no leaks that weaken your spiritual foundation.

The human body is compared to a temple—the legs have been compared to the pillars of the temple, which support the body, and the shrine is where devotion and reverence to God reside. The human head is compared to a cup of gold, crowded with thoughts of God. God created your body in his image; his Son redeems you through shedding his precious blood, and he gave you the Holy Spirit, who resides in you to lead, direct, guide, correct, and comfort you.

To survive, believers must learn to depend on God for their very being. This is revealed in John 15:5: Jesus is the Vine, and, if you have ever done any gardening, you know that the vine and the branches must be and remain connected so that nourishment flows directly through the vein of the vine to the branches. If this connection is severed, it will negatively impact the branches. Just as the branch is connected to the vine, so are we connected to Jesus. If fleshly circumstances block that connection, we cannot continue to survive; our demise is like a branch. Jesus let you know that you can do nothing without him. It is so critical for you to establish a

Accessorization

lasting connection with God through his Son, Jesus Christ. For those of you who may become caught up in the struggle of anger precipitated by unresolved issues and forget to whom you look for help to move forward, stop, take a breath, wait, and listen. Can you hear the voice of God in the stillness of the moment, letting you know "I got you" or perhaps "I got this"? You know that following God's expectations for you, irrespective of the accessories you have laid out for yourself, is critical. Learn the accessories for his expectations by reading, listening, studying, and meditating on his words. You must make time for God; you must make him your priority, holding everything sacred to him; he expects us to be accountable, and his Holy Spirit speaks to us, guiding and directing our path.

4

Jesus's Perfect Invitation Leads to Expectations for Eternal Life

Then Jesus said, "Come to me, all of you who are weary and carry heavy burdens, and I will give you rest. Take my yoke upon you. Let me teach you because I am humble and gentle at heart, and you will find rest for your souls."

MATT 11:28–29 NLT

YOU MUST ACCESSORIZE WITH commitment, completeness, compliance, clean hands, a calm mind, a pure heart, and contentment of spirit. You must be ever mindful of those personal habits that can and will put you at spiritual risk if his word does not resonate with you. God expects you, as believers and disciples of Christ, to rid yourself of gossip that may hinder or become an obstacle to another brother or sister. Sometimes, information shared in the body of Christ from a fleshly perspective needs to be validated before it is shared. You must clear your heart and mind from the fleshly judgment you pass on to each other in a simple conversation. Do not lend yourself or be a participant in fleshly judgment. It can

Accessorization

backfire, causing you to stumble or become a stumbling block in the body of Christ.

God expects you to obey and follow his commands consistently to reap the benefits he provides. As noted in Jer 7:23, he instructs you to obey him, and he will be your God, and you will be his people. However, if you choose to do your own thing, being stubborn, self-reliant, self-centered, and self-directed, then he, as your Father, who references Deut 28:15–20, will cause you to be confused. He will surely rebuke everything you do or consider doing until you are consumed by self-destruction (life-altering). While God allowed this to happen, it is your self-acting, fleshly, and disobedient actions that open the door to your self-demise.

Why do you waste so much time calling on the holy and righteous name of the Lord and yet refuse to follow his expectations and instructions? Like the garden of Eden trio, each blamed the other for their circumstance. You bury your sins of wrongdoing behind some dark web, anticipating that no one will ever know the real you. However, someone else comes along, a bit sharper than you, and cracks the web, letting your dirty, filthy rags flow in the wind and bright sunshine. Some modern individuals have taken great care and invested considerable funds to hide their secrets, but hackers are always a step ahead. As your foreparents always said, "What happens in the dark of night will surely come out in the light."

As members of the body of Christ, you cannot allow yourself to become snared in Satan's trap, perpetuating anger, deceit, jealousy, envy, and negative attitudes. You must ensure that you are clothed in God's word, wrapped in his suit of armor, and accessorized with and by the power and presence of the Holy Spirit. The Spirit God gave you to indwell within each believer is the spiritual agent by which you are strengthened inwardly to face life's challenges. This Spirit is a shield that protects you on your road to eternal life, just as the fleshly shield used by the enemy protects his servants (1 Cor 6:19–20).

Honor the Spirit God gave you to dwell within the temple of each believer. This Spirit is the spiritual accessory by which you are strengthened inwardly to face life's challenges and

Jesus's Perfect Invitation Leads to Expectations for Eternal Life

disappointments. This Spirit is a shield that engulfs you to protect you, just like the fleshly shields used outside to accentuate the self. God's eternal shield protects you as you journey in this life on your way to eternal luxury in the arms of God, with streets of gold and no worries, tribulations, or tears of despair. Be like the third little pig, build your spiritual house on a solid foundation, and the winds and rains of time, the challenges and circumstances of life, cannot destroy you. They may temporarily cause setbacks, but your faith and trust in God are founded and grounded in his holy word, and nothing can take it away.

Under the section "Teach Me," the psalmist (Ps 119) asks God to teach him his statutes so that he can obey them. Do you ever stop and ask God to teach you, or are you afraid of what the lesson may implicate or reveal about you? When God helps you and shows you the way through the Holy Spirit, do you stop to thank him for all he has done for you now and in past circumstances? Or are you taught and shown by challenges, and when the angry sea is calm, you forget about the magnitude of the storm? When life is darkest, you hold firm, and when the light appears, you may let God, prayerfully, for just a little while. Perhaps you are like Peter; as long as your eyes are focused on God, you are OK. But the minute you look beyond or something catches your attention, you let go, yet God is still there. He reaches through the waters, finds your trembling hands, and pulls you through.

A sure way to be a beneficiary of Jesus's invitation is to engage in spiritual cleansing, ridding yourself of all unnecessary accessories that do not promote spiritual growth or development, or enhance your walk as a believer. Eliminate worldly clutter and organize your spiritual life closet so it is pleasing and presentable to God. Evaluate what can be tossed as baggage, weighed down by junk without authenticity in God's service. You tidy up your inner self to become a role model and example of Christian character and lifestyle change, which can be beneficial in God's kingdom. Let yourself become habitual and forthcoming as you persist in ridding yourselves of life's backpack syndrome. Never throw anything out; instead, accumulate more unnecessary items that eventually

Accessorization

cause a hole in the backpack. You must repent of those things you do and say that are not of Christ. There is a sure possibility that those harmful accessories may be a starting point for your physical and emotional ailments. You forge ahead, always wanting to be in charge and never wanting to share or delegate some of the responsibilities hurled at you. You give the appearance that you can handle anything because of the assumption that you have a trailblazing map behind you that provides the assurance that you are OK. It is OK to abase a sister and beat her up; each time you do it, the ego becomes more puffed up. If you stop and think, you'll find yourself on an emotional roller coaster. With each circle, your health suffers, causing aches and pains, migraines, stomach ulcers, hair thinning, bulges in the stomach, accumulation of unnecessary accessories, and a messy house, all contributing to deteriorating health challenges.

Refer to the diagram on the following page, which outlines the occasions for developing a more positive "you." Do you think that you fall short in any area?

Jesus's Perfect Invitation Leads to Expectations for Eternal Life

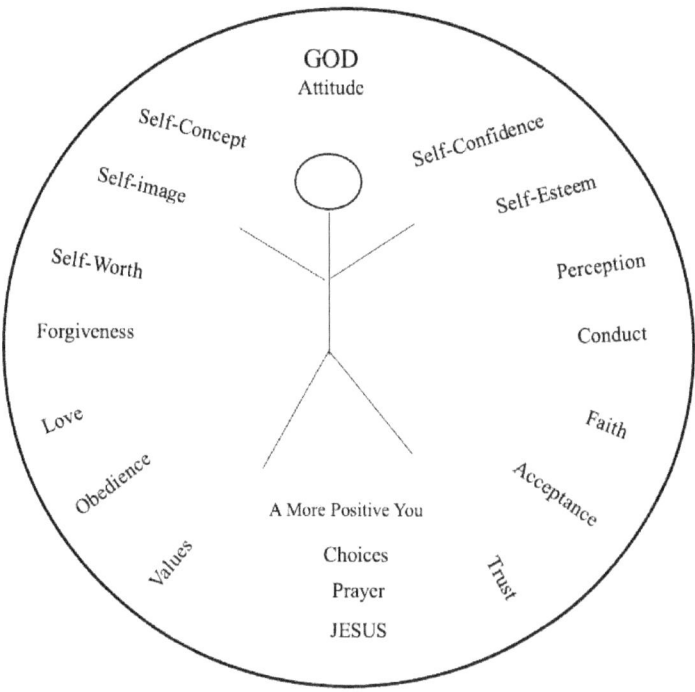

Accessories for Developing a Positive You

These accessories help individuals grow and develop into emotionally healthy adults. These accessories and feedback shared within your family, school, church, or community enable you to become healthy adults and spiritually developed, mature believers. Clarke refers to these as "fate, choices, life positive offerings for being capable and doing well, and the fourth is negative messages."[1]

---

1. Clarke, *Self-Esteem*.

Epilogue

THIS IS MY SECOND book, and like the first, *Kept: A Commentary on God's Providential Care in the Journey of a Plantation Girl*, I trust it will guide someone in the art of accessorization—the time spent beautifying the outward self and sometimes forgetting about the totality of the inner self. While God has many expectations for your spiritual growth and development (as written in Rom 14:12), he does not expect you to cause another to stumble. Are you feeling weighed down? I challenge you to try God; he will help you through your challenges, lift you from your burdens and invisible snares, and promote, through faith, strength to endure whatever obstacles man may place in your path. Being with God produces regularity in prayer and spiritual growth, and these accessories give you the fortitude you need to navigate the twenty-first century. You have experienced, witnessed, and been challenged by numerous obstacles and untruths in the political realm. It makes one wonder, where did you place God? Is he in your inner being, or have you put him aside so that you can override your conscience and do the unthinkable? Today's political system bears little resemblance to its past; lying, dishonesty, deceit, and trickery are now prevalent and no longer confined to closed doors. It makes one wonder how many people still believe that God is everywhere at once (omnipresence) and that he sits high above the earth he created centuries ago, looking down.

These are a few of God's expectations; how many have you broken or overlooked? Can you count the cost of disobedience and

Accessorization

failure to follow God's expectations? As you asked yourselves, what life-altering challenges have you faced? Have you kept his commandments, obeying him and not putting any gods before him? Have you inadvertently used his name in an ungodly way? Do you respect the Sabbath, keeping it holy as it was in previous years when "blue laws" did not allow alcohol to be sold or businesses other than "mom and pop" stores, to be opened on Sundays? God speaks of unconditional love and requires that we love one another as he loves us. Do you have this kind of love? Are you obedient to his will and his way, and abide in him as you continue to seek his blessings?

God expects you to be obedient, to trust him, and allow him to lead you safely and gently without self-obstruction. He expects you to wear the armor he has provided in Ephesians so that you are spiritually equipped to fight against the evil that lurks in this world and hinders his children. You have a generous, thoughtful, compassionate God who shows you favor. You, however, fall short because you want to be in charge without consequences; you wish to impart self-direction without repercussions, going in any direction like sheep who wander off the hillside when they leave their master behind. When you wander, you fall short and can't face the challenges, obstacles, and roadblocks set up by the world to throw you offtrack. You then call on God when you hit a seemingly insurmountable obstacle—a dark, rock wall. He has mercy on you, and through his grace, he helps you find your way.

Accessorization for spiritual growth and development may include praying, healing, meditating, and studying the word of God. What is God looking for and expecting in his accessorized children? He expects you to be fruit-bearing and spiritually empowered by accessing your minds through reading and studying his word, putting him first and foremost, and knowing that your body is his temple. You should keep it pure, clean, and holy, and not allow any muck and mire to invade and defile its chambers, the most valuable part of the body, its spirit.

God blessed you with his favor and divine power, carried you through all the weapons that were formed against you, tore you up, tore you apart, and tried to block you from calling on him, but

Epilogue

God reached through the dark mist, caught and rescued you. You must understand that disobedience can have consequences that may cause life-altering changes. Therefore, you must obey him and follow his commands to guide you in your life. God expects you to relate to one another nonjudgmentally and experience the beauty of his grace and mercy, his favor that enhances your life each day through your Lord and Savior, Jesus Christ. It is easy to pass judgment on another believer; you can see wrongdoing in their life, but fail to see the red spots hiding beneath the skin that covers your eyes or hidden from full view by dark and glare-free sunglasses. You may become a society of believers who are working toward perfection, know the complete circumstances of another, and do not stand in judgment by pointing fingers at perfection. A member has been tithing faithfully, but their financial circumstances have changed, and funds are unavailable. What does God expect of you? Are you to hold your brother in contempt because he did not give to the church as he previously did? Should you pray and ask God to show you how to approach him to determine if things are OK? Should you make a general announcement that the meager amount he is giving is not commensurate with what you think his expected earnings are? How do you hold your spiritual brother up? Imagine his circumstances. It could easily be you!

God has brought you through many trials and tribulations, and as stated in Ps 34:18 (NIV), "The Lord is close to the brokenhearted and saves those who are crushed in spirit." Please remember that God knows the intricacies of your heart and fully understands your feelings and emotions. You have journeyed through the garden of Eden, witnessed the anger and frustration of an aggressive driver, and seen the disappointment of a coworker or co-worshiper. You have also come to understand the complete protection of the armor of God and have experienced being a change agent for Christ. These accessories, whether positive or negative, serve as stepping stones to receiving your fully accessorized regalia: a white robe, a gold crown, and silver slippers, all suited for your final journey. Is your lifestyle commensurate with his requirements for you to enjoy eternity with him?

Bibliography

Abraham, Lauren. "Weekly Devotional: The Armor of God—Breastplate of Righteousness." Grand Canyon University, May 20, 2016. https://www.gcu.edu/blog/spiritual-life/weekly-devotional-armor-god-breastplate-righteousness.

The American Heritage Dictionary. "Anger." https://ahdictionary.com/word/search.html?q=+ANGER#:~:text=Anger.

Benware, Paul, N., Survey of the New Testament, Revised, Chicago: Moody, 1990.

Bible Hub. "2375. thureos." https://biblehub.com/greek/2375.htm.

———. "Guard Against a Hardened Heart." https://biblehub.com/topical/g/guard_against_a_hardened_heart.htm.

Blackaby, Henry, et al. *Experiencing God: Knowing and Doing the Will of God.* Brentwood, TN: Lifeway, 2023.

Bray, Bethany. "Self-Esteem: Tending to the Roots and Branches." Counseling Today, April 2022. https://www.counseling.org/publications/counseling-today-magazine/article-archive/article/legacy/self-esteem-tending-to-the-roots-and-branches.

Caner, Mark E. "Spiritual Meekness: An Imperative Virtue for Christian Leaders." *Inner Resources for Leaders* 3 (2010). https://www.regent.edu/journal/inner-resources-for-leaders/spiritual-meekness-a-virtue-for-christian-leaders/.

Clarke, Jean Illsley. *Self-Esteem: A Family Affair.* New York: Harper & Row, 1978.

Collins Dictionary. "Accessorize." https://www.collinsdictionary.com/us/dictionary/english/accessorize.

———. "Expectation." https://www.collinsdictionary.com/us/dictionary/english/expectation.

———. "Fury." https://www.collinsdictionary.com/dictionary/english/fury#google_vignette.

———. "Hostility." https://www.collinsdictionary.com/us/dictionary/english/hostility.

———. "Rage." https://www.collinsdictionary.com/dictionary/english/rage.

Bibliography

Cook, Stephen L. "The Temple in the Christian Bible." St. Andrews Encyclopaedia of Theology, August 10, 2023. https://www.saet.ac.uk/Christianity/TheTempleintheChristianBible.

Davey, Stephen. "What Is the Biblical Meaning of Long-Suffering?" Wisdom International, June 3, 2022. https://www.wisdomonline.org/blog/long-suffering/.

Freudenrich, Craig. "How Muscles Work." https://health.howstuffworks.com/human-body/systems/musculoskeletal/muscle.htm.

Hunt, June. *Anger: Facing the Fire Within*. Torrance, CA: Aspire, 2013.

Institute in Basic Life Principles. "Gentleness vs. Harshness." https://iblp.org/character/gentleness/.

International Standard Bible Encyclopedia Online. "Fury." https://www.internationalstandardbible.com/F/fury.html#:~:text=fu'%2Dri%20(alastor%2C%20%22,Future%20→."

Jackson, Violet. *The Art of Accessorising: Adding Flair to Your Outfit*. Kindle ed. N.p., 2023.

Kang, Joshua Choonmin. *Deep-Rooted in Christ: The Way of Transformation*. Downers Grove, IL: InterVarsity, 2007.

Katella, Kathy. "Long COVID Brain Fog: What It Is and How to Manage It." Yale Medicine, May 29, 2024. https://www.yalemedicine.org/news/how-to-manage-long-covid-brain-fog.

Longman. Dictionary of Contemporary English. "Public Image." https://www.ldoceonline.com/dictionary/public-image.

McCoy, Daniel. Sword of the Spirit: How the Word of God Puts Satan on Defense. https://renew.org/sword-of-the-spirit/.

Merriam-Webster. "Accessorize." https://www.merriam-webster.com/dictionary/accessorize.

———. "Correction." https://www.merriam-webster.com/dictionary/correction.

———. "Dismayed." www.merriam-webster.com/dictionary/dismayed.

———. "Expectation." https://www.merriam-webster.com/dictionary/expectation.

———. "Faith." https://www.merriam-webster.com/dictionary/faith.

———. "Gentleness." https://www.merriam-webster.com/dictionary/gentleness.

Montessori, Maria. "Social Grace, Inner Discipline and Joy . . ." AZ Quotes. https://www.azquotes.com/quote/865380.

Mulholland, M. Robert Jr. *Invitation to a Journey: A Road Map for Spiritual Formation*. Expan. ed. Downers Grove, IL: InterVarsity, 2016.

Oxford Learner's Dictionaries. "Accessorize." https://www.oxfordlearnersdictionaries.com/us/definition/english/accessorize#google_vignette.

———. "Self-Absorption." https://www.oxfordlearnersdictionaries.com/definition/english/self-absorption.

Plato. *Laws*. Translated by Benjamin Jowett. N.p.: MIT Classics, 2013. https://classics.mit.edu/Plato/laws.5.v.html.

Sterk, Andrea E., and Peter Scazzero. *Christian Character*. Downers Grove, IL: InterVarsity, 1999.

Bibliography

Sun, Andreas. *Master Anger Management for Success: Transform Emotions into Excellence and Workplace Tensions into Triumphs.* N.p.: Serene Turtle, 2024.

Turner, Johnny. *A Biblical Theology of Christian Discipleship.* Eugene, OR: Wipf & Stock, 2021.

———. *God Is A Strong Shelter: Weathering Storms Through Reading Storms.* Eugene, OR: Wipf & Stock, 2023.

Vine, W. E., et al. *Vine's Expository Dictionary of Old and New Testament Words.* Tarrytown, NY: Revell, 1981.

Walker, W. L. "Frustrate." Bible Study Tools. https://www.biblestudytools.com/dictionary/frustrate/.

Wikipedia. "Funnel." August 21, 2025. https://en.wikipedia.org/wiki/Funnel#:~:text=To%20channel%20liquids%20or%20fine,transferring%20liquids%20in%20small%20container.

———. "Seven Deadly Sins." December 12, 2025. https://en.wikipedia.org/wiki/Seven_deadly_sins#Wrath.

The Women's Devotional Bible. Grand Rapids: Zondervan, 1990.

Online Resources
https://www.bethlemaster.com.
https://biblehub.com/q/what/joshua11-20.
https://www.biblestudytools.com.
https://www.cambUridgeAcademicContent:dictionary@cambridgeuniversity.
https://www.CollinsEnglish.dictionary.com.
https://www.en.wikipedia.org.
https://www.gcu.edu.Spiritual-life.
https://www.growthloop.lo.
https://health.cleveland.org.
https:// www.internationalstandardbibleencyclopedia.
https://www.Keneeshasoundersliddle.com.
https://www.merriam-webster.com/dictionary/dismayed.
https://www.regentedu>journal.
https://www.wisdomonline.org.

Scripture Index

HEBREW BIBLE/OLD TESTAMENT

Genesis
1:28	110
2:16–17	13, 19
3:12	18
3:18–19	20
4:2	47

Exodus
28	80
34:6	97

Leviticus
19:18–19	52

Deuteronomy
28:15–20	124

1 Samuel
15:23	11
16:7	7

1 Chronicles
29:11–12	77

2 Chronicles
7:14	40, 77

Ezra
4:5	55

Esther
2:10–11	75
4:15–16	65
6:7	26

Job
6:24–26	63
29:14	2

Proverbs
4:1–27	12
4:23	8
6:16–19	53
7:1–5	39
10:28	11
12:1	112
12:22	102
14:29	55
15:1–2	29
15:3	119
15:4	29
15:18	42
18:21	114

Proverbs (cont.)

20:3	115
22:4	77
29:11	48

Psalms

8:4	107
23	31
34:18	131
37:8	37, 55
51:9–10	70
119	125
119:114	81
121	93

Isaiah

26:17	20
27:4–5	61
40:27–31	24
40:31	77
44:25	55
59:17	82

Jeremiah

7:23	124
17:9	96

Ezekiel

7:8–9	41
25:17–18	52

Micah

6:8	7

NEW TESTAMENT

Matthew

4:1–11	75
5:5	102
5:22	47
5:48	2
7:24–25	104
9:10–17	103
11:28–29	123
13:31–32	76
28:19–20	91
28:19	81

Mark

12:29–30	94

Luke

6:45	70
16:10	101

John

1:12–13	82
10:1–5	78
10:10	59
15:5	121
15:11	94

Acts

6	99
7	99

Romans

1:18	63
2:19	86
3:21–22	80
3:24	89
5:1	95
5:2	101
6:19	89
7:23	54
8:1–10	91
8:6–8	108
8:7	60
8:28	118
12:1	119
12:19	8
12:21	8
14:12	129

Scripture Index

1 Corinthians

6:17	121
6:19–20	120, 124
9:25	103
13:4	97
15:27–28	42
16:13	26, 75

2 Corinthians

5:21	110
13:11	35

Galatians

5	115
5:15–17	38
5:17	10
5:21–22	115
5:22–23	10, 94
5:22	92
6:2	56
6:10	101

Ephesians

2:2	60
3	107
4:11–17	56
4:29	36, 114
5:8	90
5:15–18	90
6:10	68, 78
6:14	80
6:16	81
6:17	82

Philippians

3:15	41
3:18–19	41
3:21	89
4:7	96

Colossians

2:12–16	91
3:7–10	29
3:8	42
3:10	96
3:12–15	88
3:12–14	1
3:16–17	23
4:2	92
4:5–6	117
4:5	92
4:6	30, 36

1 Thessalonians

5:8	88
5:16–18	95

Titus

1:8	103

Hebrews

4:2	75
4:12	83
6:10–12	54
9:14	89
12:10	89

James

1:8	75, 89
1:19–20	42, 49
1:19	48
3:5–6	29
3:8	29

1 Peter

1:2	7
1:16	103
1:23	83
3:3–4	116

Scripture Index

1 John
3	28
3:20–23	28

Revelation
1:8	28
20:10	13

www.ingramcontent.com/pod-product-compliance
Lightning Source LLC
Chambersburg PA
CBHW072144160426
43197CB00012B/2234